What others have
Life-Chan

Life-Changing Verses is the kind of book _____ ...use to reach into the deepest places of your heart. Carlton Ar. _____ writes with warmth, insight, and a profound understanding not only of God's Word but also the way people think, feel, and live. Taking time each day to read a short chapter from this wonderful book can transform your life!"

> *Dr. Steven Rummage*
> *Senior Pastor*
> *Bell Shoals Baptist Church*
> *Brandon, FL*
> *Visiting Professor of Preaching*
> *Southeastern Baptist Theological Seminary*

Having been the recipient of the weekly issues of *Life-Changing Verses*, I have been deeply impressed with the manner in which the Author has taken familiar and not so familiar verses of Scripture and opened them to an explosion of meaning and application. His faithfulness to the context and Biblical Doctrine has made the study exciting. I am also impressed with his challenge in the book for the reader to apply the message to his or her daily life.

> *Dr. Marion Beaver*
> *Seniors Pastor*
> *First Baptist Church*
> *Lithia Springs, GA*

It has been my honor to know Carlton Arnold as a volunteer church member and as a staff person. In both situations Carlton was and is a man who loves the Word of God and is passionate about teaching the Word of God. With experience and compassion he is a faithful mentor to men, young and old, who want to know more of God's Word and apply biblical principles to their life. In Psalm 89:1 David wrote, "I will sing about the Lord's faithful love forever; I will proclaim Your faithfulness to all generations with my mouth." Carlton "sings" through his teaching about God's love to young and old.

Dr. Bob Jolly, Pastor
First Baptist Church Cumming, GA

This is a great book to have with you when you have a few minutes. It reduces some of your favorite verses into bite-sized chunks that you can absorb. Your life would be better if you took five minutes to read one chapter a day.

Josh Hunt, Author
Teach Like Jesus
Good Questions Have Small Groups
Talking
Disciple-Making Teachers

LIFE CHANGING VERSES ABOUT MEN

ENCOURAGEMENT FOR CHRISTIAN MEN TO
APPLY GOD'S WORD WITH CONVICTION

Carlton Lee Arnold

WESTBOW
PRESS
A DIVISION OF THOMAS NELSON

WestBow Press books may be ordered through booksellers or by contacting:

WestBow Press
A Division of Thomas Nelson
1663 Liberty Drive
Bloomington, IN 47403
www.westbowpress.com
1-(866) 928-1240

ISBN: 978-1-4908-0662-4 (sc)
ISBN: 978-1-4908-0663-1 (hc)
ISBN: 978-1-4908-0661-7 (e)

Library of Congress Control Number: 2013915937

Printed in the United States of America.

WestBow Press rev. date: 9/5/2013

Do not rebuke an older man harshly, but exhort him as if he were your father. Treat younger men as brothers, older women as mothers, and younger women as sisters, with absolute purity.

1 Timothy 5:1

OTHER WORKS BY THE AUTHOR

*L*IFE-*CHANGING VERSES, VOLUME 1* WAS published in December 2012, and Volume 2 was published in April 2013. Life-Changing Verses Volume 3 was published in June, 2013. Volume 4 will be published in 2014.

While teaching a two-year class that included one year in the Old Testament and one year in the New Testament, my son took it upon himself to digitally record each class. He transcribed these notes verbatim. They are available at www.allarnold.com. You are encouraged to visit the site to read about the Old Testament and the New Testament, especially about God's story in both testaments. If you have any questions or comments, please let me know at carlton47@gmail.com.

In another two-year class, a class member took it upon himself to videotape each lesson and transfer them to DVD. Each lesson is available for a nominal fee. Note: there is a special seven-week study of the book of Revelation that has been taught in several Bible Study classes. For more information, access my email: carltonlcv@gmail.com.

There are numerous other classes originated by the author to help Christians understand their life in Christ. These classes include: *Holy Spirit, Prayer,* and *What is Discipleship?*

Life-Changing Verses
About Men

Encouragement for Christian Men
to apply God's Word with Conviction

To my friends who have been a
part of my spiritual journey

Bill Mattheus – who taught me a lot about being a Christian Man

Chuck Mead – who is no longer with us, but God used him to strengthen my conviction and beliefs. I hope to see him in heaven

Greg Sudduth – who met with me several years to discuss numerous Christian topics as they related to how we live

Allen Bowns – who is a faithful friend with a huge heart and a deep concern for others

Roger Barker – who expressed great concern during some of my serious illnesses and provided brotherly support during those times.

Chris Cowart – who never does anything small because of his big heart

Dr. Bob Lanier – who earnestly seeks the truth and has found it and it has changed his life

Joe Falls – who accepted Christ later in his life, baptized in a lake, and tells it like it is as a great witness for Christ

Larry Carroll – who is no longer with us, but you'll never find a more Godly man to learn from

Bruce Cooper – who would give you the shirt off his back as long as you met him in Chattanooga, TN

Tim Blevins – who has helped me for years with Bible Study classes, and who could make a sack of hammers laugh

Buddy West – who is always willing to do anything to help me

Wayne Lynch – who knows how to pray and does it

Joe Matthews – who has never failed to call me on a weekly basis for 14 years for mutual encouragement and prayer

Dr. Lou Meier – who is the greatest encourager any person could have

And last, but not least,

Eric Arnold (my son) – who has graciously met with me on a weekly basis for many years

One who has unreliable friends soon
comes to ruin, but there is a friend
who sticks closer than a brother.

Proverbs 18:24

TABLE OF CONTENTS

FOREWORD

THERE ARE A FEW PEOPLE you meet in life that you never forget. They leave their fingerprints on your heart. One of those for me is the author of this book.

I met Carlton Arnold in 1993. I was being interviewed by Northside Baptist Church to consider being their pastor. Carlton and his wife were two of the 45 people in attendance at that dinner. During the question and answer time, there was a bit of a lull. Carlton quietly spoke up from the back, and said, 'I have a question. Bruce, what do you see here?' I've never forgotten the question, or my answer. I replied I see people everywhere. From there I spilled the vision God was putting in my heart for Liverpool and Syracuse, New York, and reaching people for Christ. That moment was a launching pad for the last twenty years.

We are living in a day with few godly men. Carlton Arnold is a godly man. We need many more. Though I was only his pastor for a couple of years before he and D'Ette moved to the Atlanta area, he was always supportive, encouraging and not afraid to challenge me in the right sort of way. I've had the privilege to visit and stay in their home, only to reap more wisdom and encouragement. He's always asked questions and made statements that you thought about for days, or years.

There was hardly a week that went by that he wasn't meeting with another man or group of men for breakfast to encourage them in their walk with the Lord. He was and is highly respected, and always offered godly counsel. He didn't always answer your questions, but rather pointed you in the direction of the one who would – the Lord Jesus Christ.

Carlton loves the Word of God. That is where He gets his wisdom. He loves his family, and the local church. Above all, he loves Jesus. I gladly commend this book to you. You will be blessed to learn from one of the greatest teachers I've ever known.

Carlton called me recently, because the Lord had put it on his heart to reach out and offer encouragement. He cares, and in that way and many others, he reminds me of Jesus.

Bruce Aubrey, Pastor
Northside Baptist Church
Liverpool, New York

PREFACE

*L*IFE-CHANGING VERSES ARE A COMPILATION of my personal write-ups about selected verses from the Bible. Most write-ups are only one verse and some are well recognized while others are more obscure.

They were published on a weekly basis, and the audience has experienced continued growth over the years. I have been encouraged by many to format the *Life-Changing Verses* into book form so that others might find them helpful.

This particular book consists of *Life-Changing Verses About Men*. I am excited about this men's book, as several people have requested me to do this. Volume 4 should be published in 2014. After Volume 4, I plan to write *Life-Changing Verses About God* that should also be published in 2014.

These are not "soft" devotionals where you can say that you spent time with God. I am frank and candid about the current situation of the average Believer. This is based on over 35 years of Bible teaching with the last 14 years spent in teaching the Bible through seven times.

My guiding principle was to encourage Christians to understand what the Bible says about being a Believer. I attempt to answer the question, "How does the Bible describe a Real Christian?" My main objective for each Bible verse selected was to make real and practical application to a Believer's life. I experienced changes in my life while writing many of the *Life-Changing Verses*. I have a strong opinion that conviction will occur with every Believer. To God is the glory.

You will also find each *Life-Changing Verse* helpful to get to know your Bible. I intentionally included the story surrounding the verse. Also, the way you think of your Christian life will be challenged.

Finally, a surprise to me was the use of these *Life-Changing Verses* in Bible Study classes. They are used to generate discussions about various topics. To help with the use of *Life-Changing Verses* for Bible study, I have included two indices in the back of the book to find topics to discuss. The first is a list of the Bible verses used and the second is a list by major topic.

Each *Life-Changing Verse* was written by the leading of the Holy Spirit for individual use. I pray that you will be challenged, convicted, and encouraged by each one. And from your reading these, I pray that there will be changes in your life that can be attributed to the power of God as administered by the Holy Spirit.

All writings are the thoughts of the author as prompted by the Holy Spirit. The writer's sole purpose was to see the hearts and minds of Believers directed toward God after reading *Life-Changing Verses*. May God and His Son, Jesus Christ, be honored through these writings.

All of the verses are quoted from the New International Version, unless otherwise noted.

INTRODUCTION

THIS IS A PERSONAL LETTER to the women who may read this book from the wife of the author, Carlton Lee Arnold.

When I married Carlton Arnold in June of 1969, I had many preconceived ideas of the kind of man my husband would be. I prayed that God would make him the Spiritual Leader of our home. I told God what He should do to make Carlton into the man I thought he should be.

Carlton was and has been an exceptional student, an extraordinary Air Force Officer, businessman and leader. He excelled in everything he put his hands to do. But his focus began on what he could do, not on what God wanted him to do.

Then God answered my prayers and got a hold on Carlton's heart. He was a Christian, but his life in many respects was empty. God showed him that all he needed was a relationship with Him. As Carlton began to search God's Word, He began to hunger and thirst to know more of God.

He was asked to teach an Adult Bible Study class. Anyone who has taught knows that the way to learn the most from a subject is to teach it. Carlton was no exception to the rule. God lit a fire in his heart that is still growing.

He began to assume leadership in our home, and I had some major adjustments to make in my life. God didn't change Carlton the way I thought He would. God's way is so much better. We grew closer together and closer to the Lord as we sought God's will for our lives. We asked God to help us grow – and He did.

This book is a collection of some of the things Carlton has learned as he has grown spiritually. He was mentored as a young man, and, as a mature man, he has made it a priority to mentor other men. His desire is to share the things he wishes other Christians had shared with him.

The Holy Spirit opened his mind to the importance of a strong relationship with God, with men, and with other Christians. God gave him a unique ability (through his teachings and his writings) to help others discover their relationship with a personal God.

My prayer for you is that when you read this book, you will let the Holy Spirit lead, guard, guide, and protect you. God is the author of change. He will speak to you in His words, and show you His plan for your life. God's way is perfect!

D'Ette Arnold
Wife, Friend, and Sojourner

Trust in the Lord with all your heart and lean not on your own understanding. In all your ways acknowledge Him, and He will make your paths straight.

PROVERBS 3:5-6

TO HELP YOU UNDERSTAND
THIS BOOK

BEFORE READING THIS BOOK, I strongly encourage you to read the following.

Wives, this book will not change your husband. Children, don't think that your Father will start acting differently. Employer, do not believe that your employee will all of a sudden become "Employee of the Month". Men, I have no expectations that this book will have any impact on you because men are basically hardheaded and are difficult to change. The reason I say all of these things is because the Bible is clear about life-changing events. God changes people through divine actions and the power of the Holy Spirit.

I will not accept that something that I said in this book will introduce change in a man's life. But, I do expect that the Holy Spirit will do a work in a man to make that man more Christ-like.

The way you answer, "What is Truth?" has a significant impact on how you read this book. This book is based on a spiritual view that God exists and is actively involved in the lives of all Believers. Even if you have some doubts about this, you will reach your own personal conviction by reading this book.

There are sufficient discussions about the purposes of man that will result in you, as a man, having a clear understanding about your personal convictions. You will probably not agree with everything I say. That's ok as long as you know that my source for truth will always be the Bible and the leading of the Holy Spirit. My prayer is that there will be a sufficient number of men who will read this book and make some decisions to become a more active Christian man with strong convictions about the Kingdom of God on this earth. If that happens, changes will occur to other people in families, communities, churches, and the world.

Unlike the other books about Life-Changing Verses, I have divided the 52 chapters of this book into five sections. I did this so that you will know where a particular topic fits into your maturing as a Christian. Most men want to get to the meat of things, so these sections will help a man decide where to read. However, man or woman, my prayer is that you will be led by the Holy Spirit to read this entire book and apply it to your Christian life.

The five Sections are as follows:

Section 1, "Foundations of Being a Believer ", contains discussions that form the basis of Christian beliefs.

Section 2, "The Beginnings of a Growing Faith", will help you understand what is needed to begin to grow spiritually.

Section 3, "Maturing in the Faith", are Biblical concepts that encourage you to continue to always be growing in your faith and in your becoming more Christ-like in your life.

Section 4, "Specific topics related to Men", contains some tough discussions on what a Christian man should be doing to grow deeper in a relationship with God and Christ.

Section 5, "Future Expectations", describes what God expects of a mature Believer.

SECTION 1

FOUNDATIONS OF BEING A BELIEVER CHAPTERS 1 – 12

1

TRUTH

WHO HAS THE REAL TRUTH: THE WORLD OR GOD?

And the Word of God says:

Jesus answered, "I am the way, the truth, and the life. No one comes to the Father except through me.

JOHN 14:6

I BEGIN THIS BOOK WITH a discussion of TRUTH, because all of your philosophies about how you live your life are based on either believing what the world says or what God says. Unfortunately, most men base the way they live on the world. I think it is because men are very logical and "seeing is believing" is a standard of living for them. One other reason is that the church and Christianity have become overly womanized. Men would rather abdicate than struggle with spiritual truths. These themes will be repeated many, many times in the following chapters.

The world is currently bombarded with different ways of looking at what Truth is. The Truth in this context is those foundational beliefs that a person has developed in their life that govern their behavior and influence how they make decisions. An example would be the definition of marriage. The worldview currently defines marriage as between any two adults (male and/or female). The spiritual view defines marriage as stated in the

Bible – between male and female only. There are many other issues that have been defined with those two views: world or spiritual.

I am asking you, as a Brother in Christ, to reach a conviction on the spiritual view of these issues. However, many Christians will not stand on their convictions because of the possibility of being called "intolerant". When a Christian does this, I think there is severe damage to the growth of the Kingdom of God on this earth. The Kingdom of God is defined in the Bible with certain beliefs and morals. Unfortunately, we have compromised those beliefs and morals to be "politically correct." Shame on us!

In this chapter, I want to give my own overview of history that has gotten us to where we are today with worldview thinking. This overview helps me overcome most of the worldly philosophies, because I found them empty. I hope it helps you too!

Between 350BC and AD1500, the earth was considered the center of the universe. During this time, the church and state became intermingled for the sake of power of Kings ruling over the masses. The Church defined truth, and the Church said that the earth was the center of the universe and was flat. About AD1500, Copernicus discovered and proved that the earth is not the center of the universe. He used reasoning as well as research to make this claim. Naturally, the Church took an adverse position to Copernicus, because it did not want to be found wrong.

Around AD1600, Galileo confirmed the findings of Copernicus making the Church look even more foolish. About AD1700, Sir Isaac Newton put forth the idea that the universe performed like a machine. During these years, faith was being eroded by reason. Reason was becoming the tool for man to search for the meaning of his existence. God was no longer necessary to explain the universe. By the 1800's, scientists were defining "knowledge" as only observable data; a way of thinking called "naturalism". There was little if no room for God, faith, miracles, etc.

In 1859, Darwin's *Origin of the Species* was published and secular humanism became a powerful method of explaining everything in the universe. Truth was only truth if it was discovered through reason and based on natural cause and effect.

However, people became disenchanted with naturalism, because it could not answer the questions concerning the life of man; for example, the purpose of man, the meaning of life, definition of values and morals, etc. There were many "soft" issues that reason and naturalism could not address: love, beauty, relationships, etc. As a result, there was the introduction of Modern Thought that presented the idea that everything is relative. Truth could only be defined by each individual in his or her own way. This sounds absolutely crazy to me, but that is what was taught in schools and colleges

As a consequence, Absolute Truth did not exist. Truth was defined in the mind of each individual. This worldview of thinking was soon uncovered for what it was: despairing, hopeless, and empty. What has arisen is a search by individuals to try to answer the meaning of life questions. That is why there has been a recent increased interest in the "spiritual" side of living. Man has come to the point of knowing that there is something else out there but is still not willing to believe in God.

Today, the truth is based only on things observable; this is called science. Science deals with facts that are reliable and true. Morality and religion are based on the values that are subjective and relative to the individual. Do you see the error in this thinking? Today's world philosophy separates Knowledge from Belief. Believers should have a comprehensive worldview: God's laws cover everything in creation. Are you willing to stand on this truth as a conviction for your philosophy of life?

For the Believer, there should be no separation between the things of God and the things of this world. As a Believer, nothing lies outside the realm of God. The major challenge for Believers today is to be convicted of what they believe by FAITH, and not try to PROVE the existence of and the work of God. HE is the WAY, TRUTH, and LIFE. God has addressed all aspects of man's existence, and He has the answers for all of the questions that man can ask. It is man who has erroneously tried to answer those questions without the knowledge of God.

As a Christian man, you have a decision to live every day as to the strength of the conviction you have concerning spiritual things. I'm not asking you to be a street corner preacher (unless the Holy Spirit directs you to.) I'm putting forth that Christians do not need to be wimpy or shy about their spirituality. At the same time, Christians should not be judgmental about forcing their convictions on others. The Bible says that only the Holy Spirit can bring conviction to a man.

Finally, the Bible says that you shall know the Truth and the Truth shall make you free. The lie that is believed by many Christian men is that this world can satisfy their needs. The truth is that only Spiritual freedom is true freedom that will allow you to live a full and abundant life.

I deeply pray that as you read this book that your personal convictions will become very well defined about all of the "relative" things going on in the world today. I also pray that you will become so convinced of your convictions that you will stand against all of the things that God would not be pleased with. And, if anyone asks why you believe in your convictions so deeply, you will be able to explain that there are the truths you can learn from the world that are really lies, or that you can learn from the Absolute Truth provided by God. Depending on your worldview, each of you will have a direct impact on how you read this book.

2

MAN

CREATED IN THE IMAGE OF GOD

And the Word of God says:

Then God said, "Let us make mankind in our image, in our likeness, so that they may rule over the fish in the sea and the birds in the sky, over the livestock and all the wild animals, and over all the creatures that move along the ground." So God created mankind in his own image, in the image of God he created them; male and female he created them.

GENESIS 1:26–27

...the LORD God formed the man from the dust of the ground and breathed into his nostrils the breath of life, and the man became a living being.

GENESIS 2:7

IN THIS CHAPTER, I WILL discuss the creation of Man. Many things that I say in this chapter also apply to a woman. However, I will discuss the details of the creation of the Woman in the next chapter.

In the verses above, the word "image" is a huge concept for Man, because Man was created in the image of God. It is very significant that the Bible does not say, "Let me make man in my image." It says, "in our image." Who is "our"? "Our" is the Trinity of God. If you take God, the Father, God, the Son, and God, the Holy Spirit, we say they are one with one another. The Trinity is a mysterious spiritual concept that, for me, I accept on faith. I'll leave it to the Theologians to discuss the details of the concept of the Trinity.

Other religions refer to Christians as polytheistic meaning that we worship more than one God. We don't! God is one, Christ is God with us in human form, and the Spirit is referred to as the power of God. I don't have a problem with that, and I hope you don't either.

When the Bible says, "in our image," think about relationships. What is it about the relationship of the Father, Son, and Holy Spirit with one another? They have a relationship of oneness. When you read the Bible, unity or oneness is very important to God (see John 17). Therefore, God's "image" placed on Man includes a relationship of oneness with God and other human beings. It is an essential and necessary characteristic that all human beings have: the need for God and the need for others. When you apply this to men today, there are a lot of men who just want to be left alone. It is a 100% guarantee that that person will be miserable and grow depressed. God created us to have relationships. Make sure you develop relationships!

We could spend a lot of time on that phrase "living being." "Living being" means that there is more to this creation called "man" than there is to the other animals and all of Creation. God chose to create man with a personality, with a soul, with the abilities to reason and make moral judgments. God also gave man the freedom to make decisions or free will. God gave that to man and not to the other animals. That's obvious when you look at the animal world.

Recently, science has been quick to point out that the chimpanzee has 90% DNA agreement with Man. What's interesting and not pointed out is that the mouse has 88% DNA agreement with Man. This tells me that God created everything in His own way using similar building blocks for all of life. The difference is Man has a soul or a personality, and he has been given freewill. By the way, a chicken has a 65% DNA agreement with Man.[1]

The word "formed" (also used generously in Genesis 1 and 2 with "God created...") is an interesting Hebrew word "bara." The reason it is interesting is that the only time it is used is with God and it means "something out of nothing." That's the concept behind the Hebrew word

---

1   National Geographic, July, 2013, pages 102-103

"bara." God created something out of nothing. God created. He spoke it into existence. It didn't exist before. He spoke it, and now it exists.

Do not take lightly that God created you different from all of His other Creations. He desires a relationship with you that is freely chosen by you. God wants companionship with you. Read all of Genesis 1 – 3 and see how he related to Adam and Eve. All throughout the Bible, you will find that God's relationship with you is something that is very valuable and precious. He has done everything to make that relationship possible, and, yet, man continues to reject God.

3

WOMAN
CREATED AS A HELPER TO MAN

And the Word of God says:

The LORD God said, "It is not good for the man to be alone. I will make a helper suitable for him." ... But for Adam no suitable helper was found. So the LORD God caused the man to fall into a deep sleep; and while he was sleeping, he took one of the man's ribs and then closed up the place with flesh. Then the LORD God made a woman from the rib he had taken out of the man, and he brought her to the man. The man said, "This is now bone of my bones and flesh of my flesh; she shall be called 'woman,' for she was taken out of man."

GENESIS 2:18, 20-25

IF YOU ARE A WOMAN reading this chapter, please promise me now that you will read the entire chapter as I think you will find it very interesting.

There has been so much controversy regarding the role of women throughout history. I would like to say that this is an excellent example of how man can take something that God has created and misuse it for his own flesh. This will be a recurring theme throughout this book, because we are seeing a Christian man from a Biblical perspective and not a worldly perspective.

It is clear that God intended to create a "helper" for man. A worldly man will hear that word "helper" and think of everything except what it really means in the Bible. For example, men expect women to do all of the housework, caring for children, preparing meals, etc. There is one vulgar application where man expects a woman-helper to fetch him another beer out of the refrigerator. I want to clearly show what God intended for the woman-helper.

God saw that man was incomplete and lonely. Remember in the last chapter that relationships are very important to God. God decided to make man a "helper". We have to use that word, helper, because that describes God's motivation for creating women. Read that last sentence again. We have to take out of our minds how the world has described woman-helper and put in the reason God created the woman-helper. Again, this is a spiritual versus world-view of all women. Men, we want to understand and apply God's definition of woman-helper, and not our own.

God could have picked anything, but He picked a rib from Adam to create woman. He could have picked a head, a foot, a kidney, anything, but He picked a rib. Why? Any significance to picking a rib? Where's your rib? On your side. I think that means something. I don't think He just arbitrarily said, "I like ribs, so I'm going to do ribs today." No. I think He said, "I want something alongside." Hold that thought. I'm trying to give you God's perspective on this.

Who brought the woman to man? God. Did you know He was the first father of the bride? How about that? God was father of the bride. He brought the woman to the man. The father usually does that. It's customary in a wedding.

One of the things that's very, very good to do (for those who really want to get into this) is get a book on Bible word study--Strong's Concordance is one. It is an exhaustive concordance of every word in the Bible and it tells you the original Hebrew, Aramaic, or Greek meanings behind the words. It also tells you where the word appears other places in the Bible. If you have a word that you have a problem with, you can go to Strong's Concordance, find the word in question (like "helper" in Genesis 2:18), and go to other places in the Bible to find the same Hebrew word. If you go to the other places that the word is used, it may help you understand the context.

For example, who is the help in the following verse?

Hear, O LORD, and be merciful to me; O LORD, be my help."

PSALM 30:10

Guess what the Hebrew word for help is in this verse? It's the same Hebrew word that we just read for the woman to be the helper. Who is going to be the helper here? The Lord. I want for you to think about that for a moment. Think of the worldly definition of submission-what we have been trained and brainwashed with as far as what women are to do by worldly standards. If we use that definition, what have we just done to God? Do you see what I'm trying to say? You've got to look at the spiritual definition--what God is telling you a helper is. In Psalm 30:10, God is asked to be merciful. I think that strongly implies that we men will make a lot of mistakes, and God is asking our wives to be merciful. Praise the Lord that my wife has been merciful to me over the years; more on that in a later chapter.

Who is the "help" in the following verse?

Surely God is my help; the Lord is the one who sustains me.

PSALM 54:4

God is your help! If God intended for the woman to have a certain role, a certain way of looking at things with her husband and be called "helper," what did that mean? Does this help you understand what God means when He says that He is your helper? What is the wife supposed to be? She is the helper – the sustainer of her husband. The one there when you need her there. The one that when things aren't going so right and the man gets down on himself--what's the woman supposed to be? She is to be there for help, just like you want God there when you're down and things aren't going right and there are trials and tribulations.

In my opinion, this is so different from the way the world defines the role of a woman in a man's life. Man is not complete without a woman. Women bring God-like qualities to a marriage that cannot be ignored by the husband without severe consequences. God has uniquely equipped women as a helper for man in the areas that he is the weakest. The relationship between husband and wife will be discussed later in the book.

4

SIN

TOOK CONTROL OF MAN

And the Word of God says:

Then the man and his wife heard the sound of the LORD God as he was walking in the garden in the cool of the day, and they hid from the LORD God among the trees of the garden.... And he said, "Who told you that you were naked? Have you eaten from the tree that I commanded you not to eat from?" The man said, "The woman you put here with me – she gave me some fruit from the tree, and I ate it."

GENESIS 3:8, 11-12

IN GENESIS 2:25, "THE MAN and his wife were both naked, and they felt no shame." Now they realize they are naked. What happened between "naked and not ashamed" and now "naked and ashamed"? Innocence was lost. They became aware of evil when they disobeyed God. Adam had a different look at Eve, and Eve had a different look at Adam. I believe that they had the Glory of God around them before they sinned. Because of the Glory of God, they were naked, but didn't realize it because God was with them. When they ate of the Tree of Knowledge of Good and Evil, God's Glory left them and now they have none of God's glory. They are exposed. I like that because it kind of fits how we are today. A child grows up with a kind of innocence about them.

Now, some of you may be saying to yourselves that Adam and Eve were "set-up" by God, and they did not have a chance not to sin. NO! God desired man to have freewill so that man would freely worship Him and not be forced. In other words, God had to give man a choice.

Let me ask you: what kind of creature or creation would there be if there were no temptations? Would everything not be robot-like or predictive? It is our will. God says, "We're going to make you in our image, and you've got to have a choice." If you don't have a choice, what are you? You're just worshipping and praising me, because you don't have a choice. You don't have anything else to choose from.

God said, "I want you to be able to choose." There had to be a condition that required man to make a decision. Out of all of the other animals, if an animal had eaten of the Tree of Knowledge of Good and Evil, what would have happened? Nothing. They were not created in the image of God to have that free will or decision-making or choice. Satan used the one thing that would cause man to Fall. In your life, think about your temptations. What happens? Satan will use your Tree of Knowledge of Good and Evil to get you to disobey God. That's what Satan will do.

God came in and said, "I'm going to create man to worship me in the worst of all places. I'm going to make the Garden of Eden. I'm going to make the Tree of Life. I'm also going to make all of these other trees, but I'm going to make it such that he can fall. He can choose not to obey me." Just like us today.

We have this decision point where Eve and Adam said, "We will disobey God, and we're going to eat of this Tree of Knowledge of Good and Evil." This is exactly what you do with every sin that you commit. You know better, but you say, "I choose this even though I know God said that." You have to admit this. You have to look yourself in the mirror. You have to look at God and say, "God, I did that. Of my own, personal accountability, I did it myself. I chose this even though I knew that's not what you wanted for me. That is sin. It's disobedience. That is spiritual death. It is dying spiritually and physically. That's why we need Jesus Christ. That's why we can't do it ourselves.

Now, consider this from Genesis Chapter 3. What did they do to hide their nakedness? They sewed fig leaves together. Who is trying to make themselves look righteous? Hold onto this. Who? Man. Man is trying to make themselves look righteous. Man is trying to cover up their sins. What do we do when we choose the wrong thing? "Let me cover up for it. Let me get rid of this. Let me get rid of that. Let me get rid of the evidence. Let me do this and that, so that I can feel good about myself." We can't do it.

Why did they hide? And guess what you do when you sin? You hide, and the last thing God wants for you to do is hide. God wants for you to run to Him and agree with Him about your sins, and God says, "I'll clean you up."

God created an environment where man could have a choice. Man disobeyed God. The remainder of the Bible is about God making it possible for man to return to Him as holy and righteous. It's all because of Jesus Christ! Praise the Lord!

5

CONSEQUENCES
OF MAN'S SIN

And the Word of God says:

To the woman he said, "I will make your pains in childbearing very severe; with painful labor you will give birth to children. Your desire will be for your husband, and he will rule over you."

To Adam he said, "Because you listened to your wife and ate fruit from the tree about which I commanded you, 'You must not eat from it,' "Cursed is the ground because of you; through painful toil you will eat food from it all the days of your life. It will produce thorns and thistles for you, and you will eat the plants of the field. By the sweat of your brow you will eat your food until you return to the ground, since from it you were taken; for dust you are and to dust you will return."

GENESIS 3:16–19

GOD PRONOUNCED JUDGMENT FOR THE sin of Adam and Eve. Let's look at the consequences of sin to Eve. Childbirth will be painful. I'm not a woman, but I am certain from hearing women give childbirth that it has to be painful.

What is exceedingly interesting is the second part of this "judgment": "your desire will be for your husband, and he will rule over you." Now, I don't know about you, but I love for my wife to "desire" me. That doesn't sound like a terrible judgment or consequence of sin. But, we need to know what the Hebrew word for "desire" is in this verse. It is the same word used in the next chapter when it says that sin "desires" to have Cain.

The Hebrew word "desire" in this context means to flood over or have control of. In other words, God says to women you will have a desire to control your husband. Every time that I have taught this to Bible Study classes, there is always an uproar over this interpretation until husbands and wives think it over. Women, if they were honest, will admit that they do like to control or lead their husbands. For example, my wife is especially good at controlling what I wear when we go out. I think it is in the best interest of both of us.

It is extremely important to understand that the original relationship between Adam and Eve was one of harmony. The man was the leader and the woman was the helper. They shared everything. They were seen as "one" by God. There was no conflict! We can't even imagine getting through one day without a difference of opinion between a husband and his wife. Now, the judgment makes sense. As a consequence of sin, God has said that the relationship between the husband and the wife will be in conflict. The woman will desire to control the husband, but the husband will rule the wife. Neither of these conditions are God's ideal for marriage.

The solution is for both the husband and wife to recognize these consequences. The woman must admit and confess that she does want to control her husband. The husband must admit and confess that he wants to rule his wife. In the New Testament (and, later on in this book), we will discuss this again, because God's ideal is that the husband and wife submit to one another. There is no fighting over who is the leader or controller of the marriage.

I believe this is why there are so many divorces among Christian couples. The husband and wife never address this conflict that is a result of sin. It must be addressed and resolved between the two for a "oneness" in marriage as God originally planned. Otherwise, there is so much misery in a marriage when conflict cannot be resolved. Let me say that if a man thinks he is "king" or "lord" of his wife, that man is being disobedient to God. It takes both the husband and the wife to recognize this consequence of sin that results in conflict. It takes both of them to work hard to resolve it through humility before God.

The consequence of sin to Adam is embarrassing. When Eve ate of the fruit of the Tree of Knowledge of Good and Evil, Adam was standing there and letting her do it. He wimped out on protecting his wife from the evil influences of Satan. I have much more to say to men about this later in the book. For now, husbands have to consider their wives as needing spiritual protection. Men have abdicated this responsibility resulting in the raw exposure of their wives to evil influences.

When I learned this about my spiritual protection of my wife, I was ashamed that I had let so much time go by without protecting her. I think it turned around for me when we lived in St. Louis and my wife was in some deep spiritual warfare and needed help. God had me give up everything (again) to move to Florida to save my wife. I never felt more strongly about the spiritual protection my wife needed.

The other consequence of sin for men is hard laborious work. Amen? These words don't sound too good but they are great motivators for men to change the way they view their work. The verses above use words such as "painful toil" "thorns and thistles", and "the sweat of your brow". I don't think many men would disagree with this description of the current situation with their jobs.

However, God has provided a solution to this consequence like He did for the other consequences. In Colossians 3:23-24, God says "Whatever you do, work at it with all your heart, as working for the Lord, not for human masters, since you know that you will receive an inheritance from the Lord as a reward. It is the Lord Christ you are serving."

If you will make this your perception of your job or of anything that you have to do, you will find your attitude has totally changed toward work. This will absolutely free you up from the pain, thorns, thistles, and sweat of your job. God is so good!

6

RELATIONSHIP BETWEEN GOD AND MAN NEEDS TO BE RESTORED

And the Word of God says:

"Even now," declares the LORD, "return to me with all your heart, with fasting and weeping and mourning."

JOEL 2:12

I F WE WERE HONEST WITH ourselves, most of us would not like the above verse. Yet, it is one of the most important aspects of our relationship with God. Without doing what the above verse says, we notoriously limit God's relationship with us. Let me explain.

God knows that we are a stiff necked, hardheaded, and stubborn people as human beings. Given our own way, it would not take us long to self-destruct and/or destroy everything in our lives. Every time we exert our own will to please ourselves, things just don't seem to go the way we want. When the Holy Spirit convicts us of our selfish way of living, most of us have learned several techniques to respond to this conviction without doing what the verse above says to do.

We rationalize what we have done. We were tired or we had a rough day. We frequently blame someone else or something else. This is the "blame" game that all of us have played at one time or another. We sincerely believe that our decisions are a result of what others have said or done to us. Sometimes, we even say that we deserve to be selfish. We have earned the right to have it our way. Everyone else should understand that.

All of these techniques end with a blown up self inside of us. After a while, we could actually believe that we are always right and everyone else is wrong. We know better than anyone else. It is not easy to live with someone like that.

But the verse above is God's answer to get us out of ourselves and to focus on Him. First, the verse says "even now". That means as you read this blurb, you can ask the Holy Spirit to show you where you are being selfish...trying to get your own way. Now...at this very moment!

Next, understand that God says to "return". Your thoughts have been about yourself. STOP! Think on God. Think on His creation. Think on His glory and majesty. Think...Now...about God...about Christ...about the Holy Spirit. This has to be with your whole heart. This means that you are not thinking about something else while trying to focus on God... especially, things about your self!

Then, God says to take some actions:

Fasting – this is usually abstaining from food but it could mean to fast from watching TV. It could be to fast from consuming things for yourself... the Holy Spirit will tell you. You have to decide to fast and to honor the fast. This will put your heart and mind into a focus of spiritual things.

Weeping – this is definitely not a man thing! But, God is serious about being sorrowful about your selfishness. If you have ever seen the "selfishness" in others, you know it is not very pretty. I think we could say it's actually ugly. I'm reminded of that scene from the movie, "The Lord of the Rings" where Bilbo wants to see the ring that's around Frodo's neck. When Frodo refuses, Bilbo's face contorts into a monstrous and hideous looking creature. Selfishness in others is ugly. Selfishness in you is just as ugly.

Mourning – this is recognizing that you lost something while you were acting selfishly. You may have missed a joyful opportunity with your spouse or with your children. You may have missed a blessing that God had prepared for you. When you realize that you have lost that opportunity, you mourn.

Bottom Line: God wants you, as a Believer, to be honest, sincere, open, real, and genuine in who you are and what you do. You communicate with God about who you are and what you have done. That is why God created you and sent His only Son to die for you. Don't you realize that the Creator of the universe created you for the express purpose of having a relationship with Him? Once you make this part of your life, then your life will be full and complete.

7

GOD
WANTS YOU TO KNOW HIM

And the Word of God says:

LORD, I have heard of your fame; I stand in awe of your deeds, O LORD. Repeat them in our day, in our time make them known; in wrath remember mercy.

HABAKKUK 3:2

THIS VERSE CAN FIT ALMOST any time that man has lived. We hear about the Lord and His power. The more we learn of the Lord, the more we stand in awe of what He can do. If you were like me before I was 30, I could not tell you the "fame" of the Lord. I was Biblically ignorant even though I had accepted Christ when I was 12. I wasted 18 years of not getting to know the deeds of the Lord. I am ashamed that I wasted so much of the time that God was using to bring me closer to Him. I just did not see the value in spending more time with God and His Word.

The verse above also alludes to the fact that not many people at the time knew of the Lord. Habakkuk is asking God for a renewal of who He is to His people (in our case, Believers or Christians.) If you walked into church next week and were handed a test on modern news, how would you do? If you were handed a test on the deeds of the Lord, could you clearly identify what God has done in the world and in your life. I don't think many of us men would pass.

Habakkuk asked God to make known His deeds in our time. I think we are at the same time in history. God will make known His deeds, but will we be able to understand them and apply them to our lives? You see, His deeds are spiritual in nature. For example, you may have heard about the 10 plagues in Egypt and how devastating they were to Egypt. God (through Moses) had asked Pharaoh to let His people go. We can become enamored with the plagues that were physical manifestations of God's spiritual purpose. Go read about the plagues in the book of Exodus – they are some of the most fantastic deeds of our God.

But, if you read carefully, the Israelites and the Egyptians were placed in the position that they found themselves, so that they would come to know the Lord. I find this amazing, and I know God applies the same principle today. In other words, worldly events occur so that people will get to know God.

God was releasing the Hebrews from their slavery but that wasn't God's purpose. His purpose, if you read carefully, was for the Egyptians to get to know Him. Even with the plagues, God demonstrated control of the Egyptian gods, because each plague was directed at one of their gods.

If you think about world events today (and there's a lot of them), God's purpose in all these events is for people to get to know Him. Instead of focusing on the worldly event that is occurring, God wants us to see Him at work. And, when you see Him at work, you want to stand in awe and know that God is in control of this world and everything that happens to it. He has a purpose and that is to have a strong healthy relationship with every man, woman, and child. I am amazed at His entering the three dimensional world to cause things to happen, so that we can shout, "Glory Hallelujah"! "Our God is at work to bring people to Him."

As you continue to live your life, the more you focus on God's deeds and His purpose in your life, the events of this world become very incidental. God has granted you peace that passes all understanding, because you are focused on the spiritual aspect of your life. Free yourself up with a strong relationship with God and not with this world. It's your choice.

8

CHRIST
REDEEMED YOU AS A SINNER

And the Word of God says:

"For you know that it was not with perishable things such as silver or gold that you were redeemed from the empty way of life handed down to you from your ancestors, but with the precious blood of Christ, a lamb without blemish or defect."

1 PETER 1:18-19

LET'S START WITH "YOU WERE redeemed." Basically, this means that you owe someone something, and someone else paid for it. Specifically, you are a sinner! You are a low down, no good for nothing, rotten, black hearted sinner, and there is nothing you can do about it. Your first sin cost you your life with God. You were separated from God. Your sins must be reconciled with God for you to have a relationship with God. This reconciliation or redemption was made possible through Jesus Christ.

Perishable things such as gold and silver will never be enough to redeem you. In other words, your financial giving to the church is not sufficient for you to have a relationship with God. There is no amount of money that can buy your redemption. Bill Gates and Donald Trump do not have enough money. They are just like you – a sinner. You must believe the redemptive work of Jesus Christ.

Now consider another part of these verses, "you were redeemed from the empty way of life handed down to you from your forefathers." Anyone's life lived without Jesus Christ is "empty". This is one of the best one-word descriptions about a person without Christ. Everything in their life is empty. This is handed down from generation to generation. Consider holidays: these people celebrate, but there is a big difference in their focus of the celebration. Their motive is to have a good time. Afterwards, there is nothing of value to them...their celebration was empty.

Right now, there are "empty" people trying new things to make their life happy and to give it meaning. Maybe a new TV...empty. Maybe a new hobby...empty. Maybe a mission trip...empty. Even things that look like being a Christian are empty without an acceptance of the redemption made possible by Jesus Christ.

Now we come to the "how" you are redeemed ..."with the precious blood of Christ, a lamb without blemish or defect." God requires a blood offering from people to be accepted by Him. However, there is no human being who is without blemish or defect. We are all sinners separated from God. You would have to live a life without sin to be eligible. No one has and no one can. However, Jesus showed us how to live a sinless life while He was here on earth. This is why it is so important to read the four Gospels to see how he handled people who abused him, people who disappointed him, etc. "With the precious blood of Christ" is how you receive redemption from God.

"The precious blood of Christ" is the only thing that allows us to have a real live personal relationship with God. When Christ died on the cross, he took some of his blood and put it on the altar of sacrifice in heaven. He did this sometime between Friday when he was crucified and Sunday when he was resurrected. A Biblical reference for this statement can be found in Hebrews, Chapters 7-10.

The moment his blood was placed on that heavenly altar there was a huge tremor that went through all of heaven and earth. Man could now have a relationship with God. Man was made as holy and righteous as Christ! All of the Old Testament saints could now go to heaven to be with God...their sins had been paid for.

I love this vision of Christ putting his blood on the heavenly altar, as it was a moment in time that changed everything in the past, present, and future. This is why your sins are forgiven whether they are in the past, current, or in the future. The blood of Christ on the heavenly altar...it has changed your life or it can change your life. Never forget this moment in time when the precious blood of Christ redeemed all of mankind.

Now, read the last line in each of the paragraphs above to see the importance of knowing what Christ did for you.

9

HARD-HEADED
MAN'S WAY OF
RESPONDING TO GOD

And the Word of God says:

**Therefore, I urge you, brothers and sisters, in view
of God's mercy, to offer your bodies as a living
sacrifice, holy and pleasing to God—this is your
true and proper worship. Do not conform to the
pattern of this world, but be transformed by the
renewing of your mind. Then you will be able to
test and approve what God's will is—his good,
pleasing and perfect will.**

ROMANS 12:1-2

IT'S AMAZING TO ME HOW our brains can focus on something that
happened in the past resulting in raw emotions. Someone who took
advantage of us; a bad scene with a family member; a big disappointment in
our lives; and other "bad" things can dominate our attention even though
everything about that event is over with. We keep the memories and rehash
them in our brain. **Results:** you can become bitter toward people that you
love; you can grow to be suspicious of everyone; you can sincerely believe
that only bad things will happen even in the stark reality of something
good. This becomes your pattern of thinking.

And, then, there's the future. Our brains can go in overdrive worrying about what may happen tomorrow or next week. I remember thinking of the future when I thought about my children making bad decisions; about an upcoming presentation at work that became overly important; about what could happen to my family when the company announced closing the place where I worked; or about how to overcome a sin that had negatively impacted others. **Results:** you can easily adapt a life style that always lives in the uncertain future. You miss everything going on around you because of your preoccupation of what might happen tomorrow. This becomes your pattern of thinking.

In either situation, we all can get to a point in thinking that "it's always someone else or something else that makes me think this way." Please consider that no one crawled up into your brain and is making you fret or worry. Guess who's doing it? You are. I know what you're saying now, "OK, why would I want to think about things that make me feel bad." Did you hear the "I" and "me" in that statement?

The verse above tells us that our thinking becomes patterned (or controlled) by this world. It is inevitable. This world's pattern is all about the "I" and "me". This thought process is built as we grow up as children, adolescents, and adults. You know this! Think of some other people…you can see it. But God knows this, so He says that your mind needs to be renewed. How is your mind renewed?

First, God makes you a new creation…you are born again when you believe what God has done for you through Jesus Christ. Second, God gives you the Holy Spirit to tell you the truth about everything…including the way you think. Third, God has given you the Bible to read and study… so that you can see worldly thinking versus spiritual thinking. Finally, God puts other people in your life to remind you of your thought process and God's Word.

Now, it's up to you. Do you want to change your thought process? Then, just as you accepted Christ by faith…accept God's work in you by faith: you are a new creation with a new mind; you have the Holy Spirit to tell you the truth; you have the Bible to study; you have others to help you remember the thoughts of God.

So, choose today to either live your life by your old way of thinking with expected fretting and worrying. OR, choose to live your life by the new way that God has given you so that you will know God's perfect will for your life.

10

LOVE

THE WORLD OR THE LOVE
OF GOD? – PART 1

And the Word of God says:

Do not love the world or anything in the world. If anyone loves the world, the love of the Father is not in him. For everything in the world—the cravings of sinful man, the lust of his eyes and the boasting of what he has and does—comes not from the Father but from the world. The world and its desires pass away, but the man who does the will of God lives forever.

I JOHN 2:15-17

THESE VERSES ARE PRETTY CLEAR on loving the world versus having the love of God in our lives. Note that it is us "loving" the world as compared to us "having" the love of God. It is sort of like the love of the world comes from within us toward the things in this world, while the love of God is something that comes to us. As Believers, the love of the Father is in us until we love the things of the world. Then, the love of the Father is not in us. Wouldn't it be nice if God made His love a permanent part of our lives so that we would not love the world? It won't happen! God created free will within us so that we would willingly choose Him and not the world. Therefore, as Believers, we need to be aware of the fact that when we grow to love something in this world, we will be making the love of God null and void in our lives.

Our love for this world is to use, abuse, and consume things for ourselves. The only decision regarding this kind of love would be for you to ask, "What will make me happy?" We are driven to love the things of this world, when we place our condition for happiness on those things. Some of these things are literally "things" – houses, cars, boats, HDTVs, etc. Even jobs, careers, and hobbies can become things that we place ahead of our relationships with others (spouse and children.) But, even our spouse or our children can become "things" of this world when we choose them for our happiness, and they become more important than the love of the Father. We can actually love our spouse and children deeper with God's love than the love of the world.

An example of love for this world is my early love for football. To watch football games on TV or to listen to Larry Munson broadcast for the Georgia Bulldogs took priority over everything in my life (including my wife and kids.) At the time, I did not realize that those "things" of the world were controlling me. But they were. I thought that my happiness was based on watching football games. Now, I regret missing the first 6 years of my son's life, the first four years of my daughter's life, and, most importantly, the 7 years I missed with my wife because I loved watching football games. And, you know what. I don't remember any of those games. Matter of fact, my emotions became attached as to whether my teams won or loss.

In other words, these things of this world affected the way I related to my family and others. The things of this world are made to take you captive, to give you a false sense of happiness, and to negatively impact every relationship you have. Let me repeat that: the things of this world are made to deceive you on what will make you happy. I think you can enjoy the things of this world, but don't think they will bring you happiness. That's where we go terribly wrong.

We all are in love with the things of this world…at least in our materialistic, consumer-oriented society that we live in. That's what materialism and consumerism is all about…getting you to buy something to make you happy, when it won't. That's what these verses are saying to us. All of us should admit it and move on. We live in the United States of America where life is good. When I say "good", I mean as compared to other places in this world where finding something to eat is to survive for one more day. At the same time, there are people who have forsaken the comforts of living in America to live in other places not so pleasant just to demonstrate to others the love of God.

There are a few who have given up much to work in inner cities and other tough places to live even in the U.S. But, most Believers are very content to stay where they are. Why? Quite frankly, we love the things of this world. If Believers practiced these verses where they lived (even in the U.S.; even in the community you live in), there would be many who would turn to God, because they would see Believers who have the love of God in their lives.

God has a love that He wants to give to each of us. It is interesting that the most famous verse from the Bible that is seen every year on national TV is "For **God so loved the world** that he gave his one and only Son, that whoever believes in him shall not perish but have eternal life." You know this as John 3:16. His love is a decision to love us unconditionally. You see the love of the Father has an object in mind and that object is us – you, me, and every single human being. His love for the world was for us. He literally sacrificed Himself for you. And, He wants you to love others with His love.

Our love for the things of this world is not for others – it is for us and that creates all kinds of relationship problems. In the next chapter, we will consider the "cravings", "lust", and "boasting" that result in damaged relationships and an unfulfilled life. In the mean time, consider what you love in this world for yourself as opposed to the love of the Father that has been given to you to love others.

11

LOVE

THE WORLD OR THE LOVE OF GOD? – PART 2

And the Word of God says:

Do not love the world or anything in the world. If anyone loves the world, the love of the Father is not in him. For everything in the world—the cravings of sinful man, the lust of his eyes and the boasting of what he has and does—comes not from the Father but from the world. The world and its desires pass away, but the man who does the will of God lives forever.

1 JOHN 2:15-17

IN THE LAST CHAPTER, I discussed the two kinds of love in these verses: one kind that comes from within us, and the love of the Father that comes from Him. Now, I want to look at what there is to love in this world, and why it is so damaging to relationships. Reread the verses above.

The "cravings of sinful man" will literally make you a slave to things of this world – you will become just like a drug addict and have to have another "fix". These cravings will make you do things that under normal conditions you would not do – you will act irrationally without realizing that it is irrational. You'll spend time and money on things that, in the long run, are unimportant. But, at the time of the craving, you are convinced that this is the only thing that will make you happy. A sure sign of the "cravings of sinful man" is when your personality changes, because somebody (including your own family) stands between you and your cravings. You say, "Nobody had better mess with me! I've got a craving to satisfy!" This is just plain ugly to see (and that's how I see myself when I was so involved with football – just plain ugly!)

The "lust of your eyes" will distract you from the beauty that God has put into this world. The word "lust" is much like the word "cravings". You will slowly become addicted to watching things that are not beneficial to your spiritual growth. These things take the form of everything seen in this world: newspapers, magazines, movies, TV, books, and the Internet. One of the most damaging aspects of the "lust of his eyes" occurs when a man gives into pornography. Let me be very clear: every lust after anything about pornography DAMAGES that man's relationship with others – especially, his wife. Be honest with yourself about the lust in you, because it is in all of us. I devote the entire Chapter 32 to a discussion of the damaging affects of pornography in a man's life.

The "boasting of what you have done and do" is a relationship killer. Too many times I've heard how a person avoids someone else, because all they talk about are themselves. I think the root problem with boasting about one self is not being aware of whom you are in Christ. As a Believer, everything about our past is over with and done. A Believer who feels that they must rehash the past to obtain the respect of others is totally deceived by this world. They have accepted the philosophy of this world that says you must take care of yourself, because no one else will. Believe it or not, I think that's a true statement! As Believers, we rest on the promises of God who loves us and cares for us rather than the moments in the past that seemed to satisfy our egos. Those moments are GONE! Leave them in the past! All they do is prop up your ego to feel superior to others. That is not the life of a Believer.

The bottom line to these verses is that we are all guilty of loving things in this world. God knows that. Yet, He continues to transform our lives from being totally consumed on the "self" in us, to one that is directed toward Him and others. The abundant life that Christ has given us is available as we quit loving the things in this world and accept the love of the Father. Consider your decisions from eternity's point of view and not from the momentary worldly pleasure that damages relationships with others. You have this decision to make every day of your life.

12

PRAYER
HOW TO PRAY

And the Word of God says:

Numbers 6:24-26 from three different translations:

"The LORD bless you and keep you; the LORD make his face shine upon you and be gracious to you; the LORD turn his face toward you and give you peace."

(NIV)

"GOD bless you and keep you, GOD smile on you and gift you, GOD look you full in the face and make you prosper."

(THE MESSAGE)

"The Lord bless you and watch, guard, and keep you; The Lord make His face to shine upon and enlighten you and be gracious (kind, merciful, and giving favor) to you; The Lord lift up His [approving] countenance upon you and give you peace (tranquility of heart and life continually)."

(AMPLIFIED BIBLE)

THE FIRST TIME I HEARD these verses was from a Pastor of a church in Athens, GA. He said it at the end of every church service. Candidly, I thought he had made it up himself. I had no idea it was from the Bible. I was more surprised when the Holy Spirit showed me the meaning of these verses as they applied to my life in praying for others.

The context is that God is describing to Moses the way the priests are to bless the people. WOW!! Now, I had a problem or a challenge. Is this something that only Pastors can do or is everyone suppose to be doing this? Was I suppose to be asking God to bless others? I had so many of my own needs left unmet. There were so many other things that I needed to pray about. Am I really to pray for others in this way?

What about those who make me sad or mad? Those who ignore me or say something wrong to me? These verses are TOO GOOD for some of the people I know! One person rewrote these verses as follows: "May the beauty of the wonder of the undeserved love of God be on you, so that it will make your life lovely too!" Do you think that this is the way all of us should be praying for others? How about praying this for your children...your spouse...your parents...your brothers and sisters...and all others? Maybe, someone is praying this way about you.

Men are either great prayers or lousy, if non-existent, prayers. I'm afraid that we leave praying to our wives or children. In my life, God put me in positions where I was asked to pray. Honestly, those early prayers were grasping at straws of what others would want to hear.

As my prayer life matured, I found myself focusing on who God is and what Christ has done for me. When I pray now I am thinking about the Kingdom of God on this earth. I think about what I am doing in the Kingdom, and what others are doing. This way of praying came from Jesus Himself. His disciples asked Him how they should pray. He answered with the following:

"'Our Father in heaven, hallowed be your name, your kingdom come, your will be done, on earth as it is in heaven. Give us today our daily bread. And forgive us our debts, as we also have forgiven our debtors. And lead us not into temptation, but deliver us from the evil one.'

MATTHEW 6:9-11

I came to realize that I needed to be praying about the things of God's Kingdom. This had a dramatic impact on how I prayed. I considered my wife and children living in the Kingdom of God, and I prayed accordingly. I encourage you as one man to another to practice, practice, and continue to practice your prayer life. Your family needs your prayer protection from the things of this world.

Section 2

The Beginnings of a Growing Faith
Chapters 13 – 22

13

SPIRITUAL WORK
GOD'S JOB DESCRIPTION
FOR A BELIEVER

And the Word of God says:

"We continually remember before our God and Father your work produced by faith, your labor prompted by love, and your endurance inspired by hope in our Lord Jesus Christ"

1 THESSALONIANS 1:3

IF YOU HAVE EVER WONDERED how God views what you should be doing as a Christian, then this verse will give you an idea. As you read the following, consider God writing your job description as a Christian.

The Greek word used for "**work**" means employment; job; vocation from God's point of view. So, what are your "employment" responsibilities to God? God's job description for you would include: get to know Him daily, seek His kingdom first, and go and make disciples – this work is produced by your **faith** in God.

The Greek word for "**labor**" means activity that is a bother; trouble; difficult; like "laboring to breathe". God's job description for you would include: deny yourself, sacrifice for others; and serve others when it's not fun or easy (when others don't deserve it, recognize it, or appreciate it) – this kind of love is prompted from God's unconditional **love** for you.

My pastor recently preached a sermon where he defined the Greek word for "**endurance**" as "passionate patience". God's job description would include: think on heavenly things–not earthly things; your life here is momentary; run the race of life with all of your strength – your continued living as a Believer on this earth is inspired by the **hope** that one day you will be with Him for eternity.

Your performance appraisal by God will occur at the end time. As a Believer, it will not be for your salvation, but He will judge your work, labor, and endurance as a Christian. Jesus will distribute rewards based on the results of this performance appraisal. (See 1 Corinthians 3:10-15 and 2 Corinthians 9:6-7.) Work on this earth as Jesus did: "I have brought you glory on earth by completing the work you gave me to do." John 17:4. Therefore, work, labor, and endure (using God's job description) to store up treasures in heaven and not on this earth.

14

PURPOSE
YOUR INVESTMENTS

And the Word of God says:

**After that whole generation had been gathered to
their ancestors, another generation grew up who
knew neither the Lord nor what he had done for
Israel. Then the Israelites did evil in the eyes of the
Lord and served the Baals. They forsook the Lord,
the God of their ancestors, who had brought them
out of Egypt. They followed and worshiped various
gods of the peoples around them. They aroused the
Lord's anger.**

JUDGES 2:10–12

I DO NOT KNOW OF anything more important than for parents (both Father and Mother) to teach their children about God. The verses above are so sad to me, since the children of the previous generation were not reminded of whom God is. They grew up thinking that everything revolves around their personal understanding of the world. As a result, they forgot about God and exchanged worship of Him to worship of other things.

In today's world, parents are way too busy to spend quality time with their children. As a result, I suppose the same thing will happen to the current generation of children...they will forget about God. For a Father to talk about God with his wife and/or children is the best investment of his time. There are eternal returns of investment that far exceed any stocks or bonds in today's world. And, God guarantees this return.

For seven years of my children's lives, I was doing my own "manly" thing…establishing a career, playing sports, and having a good old time with my buddies. I look back on those seven years, and they were all wasted. Through some tough personal crises, God showed me clearly that it was either going to be His way or my way. I had to become nothing, so that He would become everything. After that happened, my eyes could now see how precious and valuable the spiritual lives of my wife and children were. My relationship with my wife and children became the purpose of my life.

Why did I waste those seven years?…my own pride in my own self. I was blind to others. God became number one in my life and my spiritual eyesight became clearer. What do you invest your time, money, and all other resources in because of the way you think life should be? Try investing those same things in the things of God and watch God work! There is nothing in this world more important.

Let me give you an experience that I had that illustrates what happens when you invest your time in someone else. I was in a Bible Study when a woman broke down crying, because her husband was not a Christian and would not support her in her Christianity. I volunteered to meet and talk with him. On the next Church Visitation night, I went to his home and rang the doorbell. The door opened and there stood a six foot, four inch, 220 pounds man. I introduced myself, and that I was from a church. He did not say one word and slammed the door in my face. I let a couple of months go by and scheduled with his wife a visit to their home. When I arrived and the whole time that I was there, he hid out in the bedroom. A couple of more months went by, and I tried calling him. At least, he talked to me on the phone, but it was not a pleasant conversation. This went on for 2 to 3 years and, eventually, he would talk to me. One afternoon he called me and asked if we would meet for dinner. Of course. We got to the restaurant and the only table available was in the middle of the restaurant. After we ordered, he asked me to tell him the Jesus story again. As I began to tell him about sinners separated from God, big tears started to roll down his face. It became an extremely emotional moment. He accepted Christ right then. We prayed and celebrated in the middle of that restaurant. He started going to church and becoming involved. I moved away only to find out a couple of years later that he was now the Leader of the Church Visitation program. You'll never know what your correct investments may result in. But, always know that God can use anyone and everyone for His work. Praise the Lord!

15

GOD

WHERE DOES YOUR GOD LIVE?

And the Word of God says:

"But will God really dwell on earth? The heavens, even the highest heaven, cannot contain you. How much less this temple I have built!

1 KINGS 8:27

A MAZINGLY, THIS VERSE COMES FROM the Old Testament. Solomon is praying to God about the newly finished permanent "house of God", or better known as the Temple. Before this Temple was built, the "house of God" was a transportable tent. Solomon recognized that even a permanent structure could not contain God.

This Temple lasted until God judged Israel, due to their disobedience, through the nation of Babylon. Babylonian armies destroyed this Temple and carried most of the Hebrews to Babylon in captivity. Seventy years later, the Temple was rebuilt, and it became the Temple that Jesus attended and taught in.

But this second Temple was destroyed in A.D. 70 by Roman armies. As of today, the Jewish Temple has not been rebuilt. On the same site as these two Jewish Temples were built now stands the third most holy place of Islam, the Dome of the Rock. Some say that the end times will include the rebuilding of the Jewish Temple on that site. This makes for some interesting political tension in the Mid-East as well as the plans of God coming to fruition as He promised.

The relevant question for you is where does your God dwell? Is he contained in a box? Is he limited by a religious system? Is he denominationally oriented favoring one denomination over another? Is he only a citizen of the U.S.? Does he only speak English? Does he behave a certain way in accordance to what you define as "holy"?

Or, is God who he says he is? Who is he? Creator and Sustainer of Everything! He is completely Sovereign over all of His Creation. All of the rulers of the world, all of the Heavenly host, and Satan and his angels are under God's authority. He even conquered death by the sacrifice of his only Son. And, one of these days, He will throw death and everything evil into an empty eternity, removed forever from His creation. Wow!!

With the world looking like it is out of control, God is not! Let God be whom He is to you...loving, merciful, forgiving, and empowering. You, as a Believer, have been set free from everything this world tries to entrap you with, because your God is mighty and awesome. Sometime during this week, read Psalm 96...as praise to God! "The Lord reigns!"

16

YOUR HEART
WHAT IS ITS CONDITION?

And the Word of God says:

Blessed is the one who always trembles before God, but whoever hardens their heart falls into trouble.

PROVERBS 28:14

DO YOU HAVE A HARD heart? Most people would say absolutely not. Matter of fact, there are some people who will read this and become very upset with me, because I believe all of us have hard hearts. Let me explain. The condition of your heart as to whether it is soft or hard has nothing to do with how you treat others. Now, I'm positive that a lot of you don't like what I just said. We want to believe that when we do something for someone, that people could examine our hearts and say, "what a soft heart they have!...they are always giving to others!" I do not believe this is a truth from God's Word.

That's not what the verses above give as a definition of the condition of your heart. I do not believe this is a truth from God's Word...as much as we would like for it to be. The condition of your heart is your attitude toward God. Have you thought about God today? Did you think about His love for you? Did you ask Him why your life is so hard? Did you ask Him to make life a little easier for you? Did you think about how He created everything? Did you even ask if He actually existed?

You see, our heart left by itself (without God) is not a particularly good thing. It is full of greed, it is full of envy, it is full of jealousy, it is full of gossip, and it is full of a lot of stuff that God cannot accept, because it is not holy. As a holy God, He can't accept it! Your heart leaves you in a hopeless and helpless situation. At the "heart" of your heart condition is sin. Sin separates you from God. Your heart is made hard before God, because you choose to believe that you really are righteous and that your heart is right before God, as long as you do what you think is righteous. This is one of the greatest deceptions at the time that Christ walked this earth and it continues to be a great deception to many today. You can't blame anyone else…it is your heart!

Your disobedience of God should make your heart tremble. What happens in most cases is that the heart that is in us, also known as the flesh, tries to justify or rationalize our disobedience. This is where we fall into trouble. Instead of growing closer to God, we harden our hearts so that we will feel good even about our sins. Do you understand that there is in the heart of every person (including children) the motivation toward rebellion? This sounds like I'm talking about teenagers. Teens are nothing compared to us adults, and how we play mental games with our sins and our hearts grow harder.

All of us need to find the moments when the dirtiness and nastiness of our sins hits us so hard that we tremble, because we see that God gave his Son Jesus Christ as a payment for those sins. Instead of hiding them, ignoring them, putting them off to another day, we need those moments of brokenness before a holy God. Only then will we be blessed…protected from being removed from the sight of God for eternity because of Jesus Christ.

The verse begins with the word "blessed". Do you know the word that is the opposite of "blessed"? The word is cursed. Our sins result in being cursed by God. Don't look at this in any other way. It is God's TRUTH! God blesses us when we realize that Jesus Christ took on that curse of our sin from God and has now made us one with God. Our hearts remain in rebellion, EXCEPT for when we remember what Christ has freely done for our sins. It's almost like the more we can see our sins, the more we will tremble before God, and the more blessed we are by God. But, try to manipulate our sins to make us feel less guilty, and we harden our hearts, and we are headed for some serious trouble.

Acknowledge your sins (disobedience to God) as quickly as the Holy Spirit convicts you of those sins. Go within yourself to the point of trembling before a God that would judge your sin with eternal separation from Him. Again, that's God's truth. Then, become blessed by God when you realize that your sins have been forgiven and forgotten by God. All Believers must reach this point of trembling and blessedness to become any closer to God. The alternative is to grow away from God, grow closer to yourself, and have that heart of yours grow harder…that will only result in trouble. Choose to tremble and be blessed today!

17

YOUR LIFE
WORLD STUFF VERSUS GOD STUFF

And the Word of God says:

By faith Moses, when he had grown up, refused to be known as the son of Pharaoh's daughter. He chose to be mistreated along with the people of God rather than to enjoy the pleasures of sin for a short time. He regarded disgrace for the sake of Christ as of greater value than the treasures of Egypt, because he was looking ahead to his reward. By faith he left Egypt, not fearing the king's anger; he persevered because he saw him who is invisible. By faith he kept the Passover and the sprinkling of blood, so that the destroyer of the firstborn would not touch the firstborn of Israel.

HEBREWS 11:24–28

THESE VERSES COME FROM A chapter in the Bible commonly referred to as the "faith" chapter. It's full of examples of people who grew in their faith with God. Read the verses above carefully and, then, read them again. See if you can find the following:

Moses grew up as an Egyptian, in fact, as a rich Egyptian. He had everything he could possibly want. But when he became an adult he intentionally made the decision to give up all of that. He no longer wanted to live the way he had been living.

Now, watch this carefully. As long as he was living a life as Pharaoh's grandson, he was a slave to his desires and wants. To be freed from that kind of life, Moses intentionally identified himself with "the people of God" who were really his family. He became another kind of slave to experience freedom. He was disgraced in front of all of Egypt. Yet, these verses say that he did not mind this disgrace, because he saw that Christ was greater than all the treasures of Egypt. This brings up a couple of difficult thoughts.

First, it doesn't make sense to give up the easy life for a life that was much harder. People just don't do that!

Second, Moses lived 1,200 years before Christ…how could he possibly know about Christ?

It is time to reread the verses above and look for these difficult thoughts. These thoughts are the ones that will encourage us in our life as a Believer.

Why did Moses give up the "good life" for the "hard life"? His perspective changed. As he grew up in Egypt, his focus was all about himself. It was all about what he had, how he felt, what he wanted, and on and on in a narcissistic lifestyle. He was a slave to his desires and wants. His perspective changed when God revealed to him that there was more than just the "here and now". God revealed to him that there was more to life than the pleasures of this world. Moses accepted this by faith and decided to live his life based on that faith. His perspective changed to "looking ahead to his reward." This is the same for us today as we look forward to our reward…heaven. In other words, as Moses' perspective of life changed AFTER he left the treasures of Egypt, your perspective will change as you focus on what God has prepared for you.

How did Moses know about Christ? The verses above say that "he saw him who is invisible". When? The burning bush experience. God revealed to Moses that He, God, would save His people. Moses did not call the burning bush, "Christ". Moses did not call the Angel of the Lord, "Christ". Then, how did Moses know about Christ? Moses realized his own emptiness…his own wrongdoing…his own sinfulness…he realized that he really couldn't be "good". God revealed to Moses that God alone could do what Moses couldn't. Moses, by faith, accepted God's Word. Moses came to realize that his "salvation" was from God… who we call

Christ. Moses started living his life and making decisions based on that kind of saving faith.

What about you?

Do you see yourself enslaved to the things of this world? Or, do you live your life in light of what God has done for you?

Is your daily living focused on how to get through the day? Or, is it focused on what God has prepared for you?

Are you trying to satisfy yourself? Or, are you willing to forsake the things of this world to see Christ?

Ask the Holy Spirit to work in your life to the point that you decide what Moses did...the only life worth living is one that is based on faith in God.

18

WISDOM
COMES FROM GOD

And the Word of God says:

If any of you lacks wisdom, you should ask God, who gives generously to all without finding fault, and it will be given to you.

JAMES 1:5

A LOT OF MEN ARE on an ego trip when it comes to certain things that they can do. The best example I know of is when you can get two or three men who are knowledgeable about cars and engines. I am not the sharpest tack in the box when it comes to cars. When I hear these other men talking, I am amazed at how smart they are. However, it does not mean they are wise.

For example, everyone knows that the smartest people on earth are teenagers. It's amazing how much they know that you don't know. It is also amazing how they know how to operate any machinery, perform any and all tasks, and can do anything without any help. My son went through this stage. I remember trying to show him something for the first time, but he said he already knew it. He also considered me not very smart during his teen years. Someone has said that when teens turn 20, they are amazed at how much their parents learned while they were teenagers.

The world considers "smartness" as how much education a person has. We consider people smart if they have a PhD. We think lawyers and medical doctors are smart, because of what they know. People who do research have to be smart, because they are on the leading edge of knowledge. The thing about all of this "smartness" is that it always involves facts. It involves what a person has learned and retained in their brain. For example, someone smart in religion will be able to give the Hebrew and Greek meanings to words in our Bible. The ultimate smart person is the one who reads all the books ever written and is able to recall their contents. This has not been done!

Most people don't have wisdom, because knowledge is so highly valued in the world today. The world's motto could be, "Get smart...get knowledge." Today, people love to learn about the facts about things. This is a result of our dependence on reason and logic. (Recall Chapter 1.) It also shows man's arrogance, because we really and truly believe that we are capable of knowing everything. We say that there is a reason for everything; we just haven't found out all of the facts yet. Don't get me wrong, knowledge is crucial; however, without knowing how to use that knowledge, life becomes tedious and difficult to understand, because there are always other people involved in your life.

You can be the smartest person in the world, but without wisdom you cannot live successfully in this world. Why? Because real life is all about relating to others. Real life involves the dynamic and always changing character of human behavior. It involves the emotions of people and the way they behave under certain conditions. The movie, *A Beautiful Mind,* is a great example of a very smart man who could not relate to others.

All of us need wisdom to live life to its fullest. The thing that separates knowledge ("smartness") from wisdom is that wisdom is how you use knowledge. In my life, wisdom has become associated with relationships: a relationship with God and others.

In the verse above, wisdom comes from God. What this means is that God has a purpose for your life that is defined by how you relate to others using His attributes. Wisdom comes from God, when we begin to understand what He means when He says that He loves you unconditionally, when He forgives you, when He shows you grace in a situation, and so on. You gain wisdom when you see eternity from God's perspective. The "smarts" of this world suddenly become very unimportant without wisdom.

Wisdom comes only from God, because only God knows your heart and everyone else's heart. God has given you the Holy Spirit to lead you to serve others in His name. When we live with the wisdom that comes from

God, we see people as God sees them...hurting, lonely, confused, without direction, etc. Stretch yourself to become spiritually discerning about the way God sees you and others. This is the wisdom that God wants to give us generously.

His original purpose for man was a healthy relationship with Him and each other. Our "smartness" has removed God from living a life that involves others. We run roughshod over others, because of what we call our "smartness."

Begin today to ask God for wisdom. When He gives it to you, it will not be in the form of knowledge, but rather in the form of trust and obedience of who He is and what He has done for you. You will then be free to love others as God loves them, to forgive others as God has forgiven them, to sacrifice for them as God has sacrificed for you. Your life will be lived to its fullest with God's wisdom that will always include others.

19

SIN

SIN MANAGEMENT

And the Word of God says:

"What shall we say, then? Shall we go on sinning so that grace may increase? By no means! We died to sin; how can we live in it any longer? Or don't you know that all of us who were baptized into Christ Jesus were baptized into his death? We were therefore buried with him through baptism into death in order that, just as Christ was raised from the dead through the glory of the Father, we too may live a new life."

ROMANS 6:1-4

WHEN I ASK PEOPLE WHAT sin is, most people describe specific actions (adultery, murder, gossip, anger, etc.) May I say that the root problem of our sins is not what we do, but that our heart (attitude) is not directed toward God? Instead, it is directed to ourselves – what we do and what we don't do. Disobeying God is not the action you take but the "mind set" you have toward God.

We fill our brains with all the actions that we classify as sins, and then we try to avoid them. This can be called a "Sin Portfolio" that requires constant "Sin Management." If we commit one of the "sins" in our portfolio, we then spend brainpower on justifying why we failed to avoid the sin. We just keep going on sinning. Where is God in all of this brain energy?

Sin is disobedience to God. The word translated as "obey" in the Bible, means to hear with the intent to obey. What we miss is the word "hear".

The spiritual success of your life is based on you intently hearing God through His Word and the Holy Spirit.

What God says about your sin is that He will convict you of all of your sins through the Holy Spirit. He has also forgiven and forgotten your sins! To God, your sin is as far as the east is from the west. He has also cleared your conscience of the guilt of the sin. I have to ask you to think about what is left to be done about your sin? Nothing!

God has taken care of everything about all of your sins. He does not need you to "manage" your sins. When He asks you to confess your sins to Him (see 1 John 1:9), He is asking you to "agree" with Him that you have sinned. This agreeing with Him is not to obtain forgiveness, but is to recognize your dependence on God to be cleansed from your sin and to be made righteous. This is something that only He can do. This is to strengthen your relationship with God. The quicker you acknowledge and agree with the sins that you are convicted of, the stronger your relationship with God grows.

God said that King David had a "heart after God." I always found this hard to accept, because David committed some terrible sins. Among other sins, he committed adultery and murder. But when confronted and convicted about these sins, David immediately recognized and agreed with God that he had sinned against God. God wants you to recognize sin in your life as quickly as conviction occurs. He wants you to agree with Him that you have sinned, and that He has forgiven and forgotten your sins. The next step He wants you to take is to love Him and love others. He does not want your mind dwelling on the sins that He has already forgotten. No matter how bad a sin you think you have committed, it is forgiven and forgotten. Now, all you have to do is to agree with God.

Stop managing your Sin Portfolio and start listening to God. He is your Creator and Sustainer...He is all-powerful and all knowing...He loves you and forgives you of all of your sins. Why do think you have all the answers when it comes to sins? He has given you a new life. Live life to its fullest in that new life!

20

GOD

GOD IS BETTER THAN YOU!

And the Word of God says:

"My heart is changed within me; all my compassion is aroused. I will not carry out my fierce anger, nor will I turn and devastate Ephraim. For I am God, and not man."

HOSEA 11:8-9

THIS IS A FASCINATING VERSE where God is talking about Himself. It is amazing what He says. He is thinking about passing judgment when His "heart" is changed and His "compassion" is aroused. What a phenomenal thought about God's love and compassion for those who continue to reject Him and disobey Him. He has a child (Israel) who is going the wrong way, but He's having a hard time passing judgment, because He loves his people so much. He's hoping and begging that they would change and turn around. In the end, He's saying, "I won't devastate you, because I am better than man. I am God." WOW!!! Isn't that the truth!?

Normally, after being told "No" repeatedly, humans would give up and say, "I've done all I can do, and if you're going to go that route, then you're on your own." Can you hear your frustrated self saying this to your children? Or, a spouse thinking this about their mate? Even in the end here, God is saying, "You're not on your own, because I am better than man."

Aren't you glad God is who He says He is? He is not like us in passing judgment or in giving love. Man would have probably given up by now. God knows that His discipline has more redemptive qualities than punitive qualities. He's always trying to turn us around rather than strictly punish us for making wrong decisions. He wants us to turn around and come back to Him. So, He loves us and continues to love us and, then, He loves us some more. Get the picture? As a man, God wants you to see the same things in your life as you relate to your wife, your children, and others. I personally take great comfort in knowing that I have someone (God) who will help me through any crisis as a man. I can be the man God has developed and continue to rely on Him for everything rather than myself.

21

YOUR LIFE
INSUFFICIENT LIVING

And the Word of God says:

Then he called the crowd to him along with his disciples and said: "If anyone would come after me, he must deny himself and take up his cross and follow me. For whoever wants to save his life will lose it, but whoever loses his life for me and for the gospel will save it. What good is it for a man to gain the whole world, yet forfeit his soul? Or what can a man give in exchange for his soul?

MARK 8:34–37

INSUFFICIENT LIVING IS THIS: EACH day, you live your life with the hope that nothing bad will happen to you or to those you love. You pray, "Don't let anything bad happen." Each day, you live your life to make the uncertainties of tomorrow more knowable and controllable. You pray, "Please, no surprises!" Each day, you live your life trying to forget the bad things you did yesterday. You pray, "I'm not as bad as some others I know."

This is not living as God intended you to live. You are so far from the truth of what God has given you. You see, you don't live your life taking care of yourself. God says to live your life as though you were losing it. As long as you try to live your life in a way that YOU define makes you happy – you will be in a state of "INSUFFICIENT LIVING". You will always be trying one more thing that you think will make you happy.

The richest, the most famous, the most powerful men do not experience a happy life based on their definition of happiness. A constant and continually growing relationship with God is the only way to the truth about living. And that TRUTH is a Person – Jesus Christ. He is not someone you know about…He is someone who lives His life in you.

I am afraid that there are too many Christian men who have replaced an exciting, totally trusting God type of life for a life that they have found to be comfortable for them. This sounds OK but it is an extremely selfish way of living. The problem with their type of life is that, as they grow older, they will find it empty. Instead of spending time on relationships with others, they have to continually support their own definition of what life is. No man can continue to do the "young" things that we men do. Eventually, we wear out and must find other ways to find value in our lives. This type of living always includes a very selfish way of looking at their own lives even at the expense of their wives and children.

Therefore, you must lose your life to gain His life. Jesus desires to live your life in an Abundant, Powerful, Joyful and Peaceful Way. He said that He is the Way, the TRUTH, and the LIFE. Any other life including the one you try to live on you own is INSUFFICIENT LIVING.

22

YOUR LIFE
CONVERSATION IS GETTING
WORSE AND WORSE

And the Word of God says:

Let the word of Christ dwell in you richly as you teach and admonish one another with all wisdom, and as you sing psalms, hymns and spiritual songs with gratitude in your hearts to God.

COLOSSIANS 3:16

YELLING AND SCREAMING SHOULD ONLY occur when someone is in danger, and you are trying to get their attention. Yelling and screaming IS NOT an effective way to discipline children. Yelling and screaming belittles your wife. Let me say it very clearly, "there is no place or time that yelling and screaming would be a positive action.

In the past, I yelled and screamed because I was not getting the attention that I wanted. The problem was with me and not my wife or children or others. I remember when I was an Assistant Coach for my son's soccer team. One game, I started yelling and screaming at the players on the field. I was so loud and frustrated that there came a time where the other coaches, players, and parents in the stands were all staring at me. I had lost control and it was a very embarrassing moment.

Another time that the Holy Spirit used to make a life-change with me was when my son was out playing with other kids in the neighborhood. I looked outside to see how my son was doing and found the other boys with my son's sports equipment. My son was sitting on the curb not doing anything. I went livid. I marched out to those boys and started reading them the riot act.

I have never forgotten that incident, because the Holy Spirit let me see how I could have negatively impacted not only the boys I yelled at but also my son. Yelling and screaming is very hard for me to do now, because there is zero value in doing it. All it shows is something lacking in the person doing the yelling. Just don't do it!

The world's conversation is getting worse and worse. It's considered boring to say anything nice to anyone, because everyone wants to hear the "dirt" on others. We are our own worst enemy. The media is always focusing on the nastier side of people's lives. Personal conversations with others seem to always be updates on the latest "did you hear about". Even in marriages, our conversation is seen as "he said...she said". And parents continue to berate children with words that hurt, cut, and demoralize a child.

Is the "word of Christ" dwelling richly in you? I love that! Paul described the word of Christ as those things which are true, noble, right, pure, lovely, admirable, excellent, and praiseworthy. These are the kinds of words that I think should be used when describing any Christian man especially by his own wife and children.

I guess this world would be a lot quieter if we only said true and noble kinds of things. And, maybe it should be quieter! In another passage, Paul said that, as Believers, we should be kind, humble, gentle, and patient. We should bear with each other and forgive each other. I think that the amount of time we think (dwell) on these things is directly related to what our conversation is like.

In addition, we are to be about teaching and admonishing. Teaching is helping others see God's perspective. Admonishing is helping others to remember the things God has done for them. By the way, for some reason, I grew up thinking that "admonishing" meant to correct, shame, or point a guilty finger at others. I found out that the Greek word used here means to "put in remembrance". I like that!

We are to relate to each other with wisdom, psalms, and songs. Just think of the impact that Christmas songs have on people. Even secular songs can move a person. I'm one of those that would play Christmas songs all year long...they are uplifting. They tell the story of a baby in a manger who was born to save the world and to give me eternal life. That is uplifting! And, as we think on that story, "gratitude" wells up in our hearts for what God has done for us. With this gratitude in mind, you can let the word of Christ dwell in you richly as you interact with others. As the verse says, "Glory to God in the highest, and on earth peace, good will toward men."

SECTION 3

MATURING IN THE FAITH
CHAPTERS 23 – 30

23

PURPOSE

YOUR PURPOSE IN LIFE VERSUS

THE PURPOSE OF YOUR LIFE

And the Word of God says:

13 The carpenter measures with a line and makes an outline with a marker; he roughs it out with chisels and marks it with compasses. He shapes it in the form of man, of man in all of his glory, that it may dwell in a shrine.

14 He cuts down cedars, or perhaps took a cypress or oak. He let it grow among the trees of the forest, or planted a pine, and the rain made it grow.

15 It is man's fuel for burning; some of it he takes and warms himself, he kindles a fire and bakes a bread.

But he also fashions a god and worships it; he makes an idol and bows down to it.

16 Half of the wood he burns in the fire; over it he prepares his meal, he roasts his meat and eats his fill. He also warms himself and says, "Ah! I am warm; I see the fire."

17 From the rest he makes a god, his idol; he bows

**down to it and worships. He prays to it and says,
"Save me; you are my god."**

May I equate "idol" in the above verses with the "PURPOSE" of life. Early in my life, I thought that my purpose in life was to graduate from school and get a job. Then my purpose was to get married. Then it became to earn a lot of money. At one time, it was to take care of my needs and me. But, let's read on!

18 They know nothing, they understand nothing; their eyes are plastered over so they cannot see, and their minds are closed so they cannot understand.

19 No one stops to think, no one has knowledge or understanding to say, "Half of it I used for fuel; I even baked bread over its coals, I roasted meat and I ate. Shall I make a detestable thing from what is left? Shall I bow down to a block of wood?"

20 He feeds on ashes, a deluded heart misleads him; he cannot save himself, or say, "Is not this thing in my right hand a lie?"

ISAIAH 44:13-20

I THINK THAT MOST PEOPLE who read these verses can see themselves. We all make idols of what God created. For example, I took what I earned in this world and made an idol out of it. Part of my earnings I used to buy a house, TVs, a car, etc. I worked on my house and watched TV. I washed and waxed my car. I took care of it. I spent hours looking at it shine. I drove around looking for the "looks" I got from others. I thought I was the average man living the life that he was supposed to live. When the truth is discovered, all the things of this world turn to "ashes".

Then the focus of my life changed from looking at my purpose in life to the purpose of my life. I now understand that God says to include Him in all I do; to think of Him throughout the day; to awake in the morning and go to sleep at night thanking Him for all He has given me. I understand that I am to take care of my wife and children. I realized that it is impossible to earn anything in this world. It all belongs to God and should be used for Him.

All of this is to say that I am beginning to realize that everyone has only one purpose in this life: to have a deep and strong relationship with God – that's why He has done all that He has done and Christ did what

He did. I think that most Christian men would have a problem with this because of their attitude toward God and, be careful of this word, "church". I'll discuss men going to church in another chapter.

Read the verses above from your own Bible. Ask the Holy Spirit to show you what you have fashioned as an idol from what God has created and given. Then, repent (see the idol as nothing) and choose to love God with all of your heart, soul, mind, and strength.

24

PRIORITIES
URGENT VERSUS IMPORTANT

And the Word of God says:

Can any one of you by worrying add a single hour to your life?

MATTHEW 6:27

DO YOU KNOW THE DIFFERENCE between something that is "URGENT" and something that is "IMPORTANT"? Somehow or other Christians today need to make up their minds on what is "IMPORTANT" from God's perspective and what they consider as "URGENT".

Too many times we put "URGENT" stuff ahead of "IMPORTANT" things. For example, you frequently see a Father who has promised his kids to do something with them (this is called "IMPORTANT") only to bail out at the last minute because something else (yard, job, etc.) requires his time (called "URGENT"). I am including myself when I say that most Christian men have not clearly defined their urgent versus important activities in this world. It is imperative that a Christian man put God first in his life. If he doesn't, then, like me, he will be totally blind and deaf to others (including his wife and children.) I cannot tell you how much easier life has been since I straightened out my priorities.

For example, I was leading an important meeting at my work place when my assistant interrupted with an urgent call from my wife.

[Before going further with this example, I have to tell you that one huge change I made in my priorities was that if my wife called me at the office, I was to be interrupted regardless of who was in my office. I made it clear that when my wife called, she was to be treated like the President of the U.S. calling me. Men, this told my wife that she was more important to me in my life than my work. It was not easy to make that decision but it was one of the best decisions I ever made in my life. I never caught any flack from anyone at work. If anything, I think other men wanted to do the same thing!]

Now, back to the example. The urgent call was to tell me that my 13 year- old daughter had disobeyed us and was at the bowling alley with someone she was not suppose to be with. This left me in a quandary because of the importance of the meeting, my leading the meeting, and the point at which we had reached was a critical item on the agenda. I could sense my flesh telling me to continue with the meeting, and I could sense the Holy Spirit telling me how important this moment was for my daughter.

It didn't take too long for me to excuse myself from the meeting telling them to do the best they could. I told them I had something urgent to take care of. And, I did! The Holy Spirit knew the right action. It was up to me to decide on that action. No one remembers anything about that meeting (matter of fact, the business no longer exists), but my daughter (who is now 40) still remembers that day and everything that happened. She knew that I cared for her more than my job. Christian men: listen to the Holy Spirit and become strongly convicted about what you are to do and then, do it!

Worrying would cease or at least take a nose-dive if we men would decide to do the "IMPORTANT" things in life rather than the "URGENT" things. After all, "IMPORTANT" things affect eternity. "URGENT" things are done one day and replaced with other "URGENT" things the next day. There is never enough time to do the "URGENT". Instead, let God show you the relationships that are "IMPORTANT" in your life and become involved with those.

25

YOUR LIFE
WHAT ARE YOU DOING
WITH YOUR WEALTH?

And the Word of God says:

**Command those who are rich in this present world
not to be arrogant nor to put their hope in wealth,
which is so uncertain, but to put their hope in
God, who richly provides us with everything for
our enjoyment. Command them to do good, to be
rich in good deeds, and to be generous and willing
to share. In this way they will lay up treasure for
themselves as a firm foundation for the coming
age, so that they may take hold of the life that is
truly life.**

1 TIMOTHY 6:17-19

T HE VERSES ABOVE SPEAK LOUD and clear to those who have riches and
wealth. By the way, if you live in the U.S. you are probably in the top
5% of the wealthiest people on this earth. I'm not talking about billionaires
and millionaires…I'm talking about you and me…just the plain old middle
class of the U.S.

So the first thing these verses say to us rich people is not to be arrogant
about our wealth. GUILTY! GUILTY! We have all done this when we

have something that someone else does not have or if we have the latest that others don't have. We become arrogant, "look what I have and you don't!" Sounds kind of childish and that's what it is.

The second thing the verses say about all of us rich people is not to put our hope in our wealth. GUILTY! GUILTY! Again, we have all done this. The monthly paycheck is our only hope to keep our heads above water financially. Our 401K or retirement account is our only hope to live the kind of life in retirement that we've always wanted to live. Your paycheck and your 401k and your retirement account are all uncertain. You do not know what tomorrow may bring.

But the verses tell us to put our hope in God who is the real source for our enjoyment. I can hear some of you saying that you have always wanted a boat. You could tell God that a boat would bring such enjoyment to you and your family and friends that you let ride on your boat. Certainly, that's an enjoyment that God intended. Recall the title for this write-up, "What are you doing with your wealth?" How do you spend your wealth? Is it to buy all the things that everyone else has so that you will feel important? Is it to buy something because, quite frankly, you deserve it! You see, God does not get involved in becoming a CPA for your finances. He wants you to know where your wealth came from…God! And, He wants you to use that wealth so that He will be glorified.

One mind set that bothers me about our wealth in the U.S. is that we think we are suppose to spend all that we make on ourselves. We may give some to charities and our church, but all the rest belongs to me. I can do with it as I want. I do not think that is Biblical simply because it is so selfish. The following Biblical passage is from Acts 2:44-45:

All the believers were together and had everything in common. They sold property and possessions to give to anyone who had need.

I'm not trying to read more into these two verses than there is, but it seems to me that part of the "left-over" of your paycheck should be set aside to share with others in need. It's like this. God blesses you with an income. You tithe to your church and maybe give to a charity. I think God is asking more of you. Set aside some money out of your income to help others who become in need. This principle has never been more needed than the last economic downturn. Don't believe you have to spend all of your income. Save some for others. I believe this is a Biblical principle that very few Christians follow. We all need to do a better job.

The other Biblical principle about wealth that Christians seem to ignore is to not get into debt. This is where you spend more money than you receive. You become a slave to debt. God does not want you to be a slave to debt but a slave to Him. Also, debt is one of the major stresses in marriages. When either the husband or the wife are not financially responsible, it is up to the husband, as the spiritual leader of the home and accountable to God for his family, to get his own finances in order and/or to help others in the family get control of their spending.

As a side note, there is an agreement that my wife and I reached regarding our finances. Finances are a major problem in marriages today because of over-spending to live a higher quality of life. Unfortunately, someone has to pay for these debts. God gave my wife and me an understanding that we were not to talk about finances after 9:00PM. This simple rule in our home greatly changed our relationship and our ability to get a good sound sleep at night. The other thing that God showed us was to work together on any purchase by limiting what each could spend without the other's approval. Our limit was $100. Anything over $100 required the approval of both of us. This was another extremely helpful rule that we both followed. We both submitted to this principle with complete agreement and no exceptions. Eventually, we became debt-free, and I cannot tell you how great she and I felt about how we jointly handled our finances. What is gloriously amazing and we praise God for it that when we want to give money to someone, we separately come up with a dollar figure and it is always the same. God has truly made my wife and I "one flesh" when it comes to money. I hope rules like the above are active in your marriage. They will set you free.

Read the verses again. The rich, that's you and me, are commanded to do good by being rich in good deeds. These good deeds are very specific: be generous and be willing to share. By doing this, Believers will be investing in a "firm foundation for the coming age". PLUS, we will be taking hold of the life that is truly life.

26

Your Influence
You are a pleasing
aroma of Christ

And the Word of God says:

But thanks be to God, who always leads us as captives in Christ's triumphal procession and uses us to spread the aroma of the knowledge of him everywhere. For we are to God the pleasing aroma of Christ among those who are being saved and those who are perishing. To the one we are an aroma that brings death; to the other, an aroma that brings life.

2 CORINTHIANS 2:14-16

THESE ARE WONDERFUL VERSES FROM God's Word, and I hope you will read this carefully.

It is strange wording to call us as "captives" but it reinforces the idea that we now belong to God and not the world, and definitely not Satan. Christ leads us in a victorious parade demonstrating to all onlookers the joy and peace that we experience, because we belong to God. If you have ever experienced being in a parade, it is exciting as you recognize some people who are watching the parade. There is an exchange of recognition either by pointing or saluting or throwing things at them (e.g., candy). I want you to see yourself in this procession with Christ leading. More importantly, I want you to picture your life as a continuous participant in this procession of victory because of what Christ did on the cross. You are identifying yourself to everyone watching that you are a child of the King and that He has given you riches beyond anything imaginable.

These verses also speak loudly about how God sees your life here on this earth as it influences others. God uses you, as a Believer, to spread the aroma of the knowledge of God everywhere. You don't have to do anything. God uses your life to show others who He is. God calls this an aroma. I think of aromas in two ways. The first way is the smell of a beef roast cooking in the oven that is very pleasing to smell. As a matter of fact, such an aroma awakens my sense of hunger. All of a sudden my appetite becomes very strong, and I start looking forward to partaking of that roast.

The second way I consider aroma is a stinking odor. We recently stayed in some cabins at a campground and, unfortunately, there was raw sewage leaking from the ground near the cabin. It was a terrible odor that made me nauseous. I wanted to get away from that smell as quickly as possible. Even after I removed myself from smelling the stinking stuff, I continued to smell the odor, because it had been so strong. Needless to say, it took away my appetite and ruined a perfectly beautiful morning sitting in a rocker on a porch looking at a lake.

Please consider this about you and your aroma from God. To God, you are a pleasing aroma of Christ among those who are being saved. As I have grown older, my need to fellowship with brothers and sisters in Christ is stronger than the aroma of a beef roast cooking. There is pleasantness about being with other Believers. They, in turn, experience that same strong sweet smelling aroma from your life. The aroma is self-sacrifice. The aroma results from praising God and thanking Christ for His forgiveness of our sins. This is a part of every Believer's life that should not be taken for granted but should be experienced to its fullest. It happens so often in corporate worship with other Believers and the study of God's Word with others. This kind of aroma brings every Believer LIFE! There's nothing on this earth that can beat it.

However, just like there is the sweet smelling aroma of life for the Believer, there is also the stinking aroma that those without Christ experience. This aroma is called death. I don't know of many things that smell worse than a rotting corpse or rotten meat. If you understand this spiritual principle about the stinking aroma of death, then you know that when you are in the presence of unbelievers, you are not pleasant to be with. It is not you but the prospect of eternal death. This principle should answer all of your questions and concerns on why some family members and friends do not want to associate with you. It's not you, but it is the aroma of eternal life – Jesus Christ.

I want to share a story about a man who became a good friend of mine. I worked for him for four years. He was known as the "manager from another planet" by anyone who knew him. He came by that name honestly. He was arrogant, egotistical, narcissistic, sacrilegious, an atheist, etc. It was extremely hard to work for him until God showed me that I was the only living being that could share Christ with him and he would listen. At the same time, my convictions grew stronger because of the talks we had. He would do anything to try to shake my faith, but God showed me my purpose with Him and empowered me through the Holy Spirit to remain friends with him. For some reason, he spent a lot of time with me in going to lunch and on business trips. I witnessed to him more times than I can count. During this time with him, God strengthened my convictions about my beliefs. I almost wish everyone had a "manager from another planet" to befriend and be able to witness to them.

I pray that that these words will encourage you to always associate with other Believers. I also pray that you associate with unbelievers so that they might see the joy and peace that you have, because you have eternal life with God. The unbelieving onlooker of the procession that you are in that is led by Christ will smell the stink of death. I know the Holy Spirit will convict that person of that truth, and the person will have the opportunity to accept Jesus Christ. In the mean time, keep smelling good with the sweet aroma of Christ.

27

SATAN

MEN: PROTECT YOUR FAMILY

And the Word of God says,

**The thief comes only to steal and kill and destroy;
I have come that they may have life, and have it
to the full.**

JOHN 10:10

THE CONTEXT OF THIS VERSE is Jesus talking to the Jewish religious
leaders about a shepherd and his sheep. He refers to Himself as the
Great Shepherd and those who believe on Him as His sheep. What is
significant about this verse is the sharp contrast of words used in the verse.
I believe that men should always be aware of Satan's attacks on his family.
The man is not only the spiritual leader of the family but also the spiritual
protector. I am afraid most Christian men have neglected both of these
responsibilities to their families.

The "thief" could be one of several things or all of one something. I
believe that the "thief" is Satan. The other things that the thief could be are
all motivated by the evil work of Satan. For example, if the thief were false
Messiahs (and there were plenty of them running around), then I would
say that Satan influenced them. If the thief were the religious rulers, the
same thing holds. No matter whom you select as the thief, it will always
come back to the evil work of Satan.

Another indication that it is Satan is that his only purpose was to "steal and kill and destroy." When Satan was expelled from heaven by God (see Isaiah 14:12-15 and Ezekiel 28:17), I believe that Satan threw a major temper tantrum. He threw everything he had against what God had created. As an example, he literally tried to steal, kill, and destroy the Jews on several occasions throughout Jewish history. The book of Esther is one example, and the holocaust is another example. Satan is in the stealing, killing, and destroying business. We, as Christians, do not need to give him the slightest foothold into our lives.

The world today is all about stealing, killing, and destroying. For example, some of the most popular electronic games are those that allow the participant to kill and destroy monsters, aliens, and even human beings. The news is always full of stealing, killing, and destroying. TV shows and movies have become so graphic with stealing, killing, and destroying. All of this worldly stuff will eventually get into people, families, and nations.

When it comes to you, specifically, Satan wants to steal, kill, and destroy you and your family, because you represent God. Satan and his demons try very hard to steal your joy and peace. He will do anything he can to make you depressed, angry, sad, mad, and the list goes on. Don't let him do it! Satan kills when he convinces someone to go against the commands of God or parents or anyone in authority. What dies is who you are in Christ. Your priorities, values, and morals will be sacrificed, because you'll think that you have a right to do what you want to do. Satan will take advantage of your busyness to kill your reading and studying the Word of God. Finally, Satan destroys relationships with others. Families are torn apart and destroyed when Satan can introduce rebellion into a family. The love between husband and wife can be destroyed with the lies of Satan. He is a deceiver.

Now, here comes the good part. Jesus says in the second part of the verse above that He came so that you and I can have life and have it to its fullest. Another translation for the full life is an abundant life. That sounds a lot better than stealing, killing, and destroying. I think you can see the sharp contrast from the work of Satan in this world and what God has done for you. It's interesting that even though we live in the world that is currently Satan's domain, Jesus says that we can live a full life in the here and now. It's amazing to me that Believers can live a life like that on this earth. But, that's the whole point of God sending His Son to die for you and to free you from all of the broken parts of this world. That's why He has given you the Holy Spirit to help you fight the spiritual battles that Satan and his demons use to steal, kill and destroy.

Satan has no hold on you to steal, kill, and destroy anything you have, unless you allow it. On the other hand, the abundant life is exactly what God wants you to have. Why? Not for you! It is so that others might see Christ in you. Again, Satan wants chaos and rebellion in this world. We, as Christians, should not allow this chaos to control our emotions and our thoughts.

To live the abundant life is to think on the Almighty God and His work in your life. Think about those things that are in heaven and live the abundant life. Think on your fellowship with other Believers and live the abundant life. Let's all help one another to stay focused on Jesus Christ as our Great Shepherd, who loves us and died for us. Stop dwelling on the chaos, hopelessness, and filthiness of this world.

I know what I am about to say will hit most of you up-side the head with a 2x4. Have you ever considered that the news you watch on TV and read in the newspaper is all about stealing, killing, and destroying? In other words, the results of Satan's work on this earth are being reported to you! There is not much news reported that is not generated by Satan and his demons. You may not like to hear this because you love the news, and it's a way to find out what is going on in this world. I rest my case…it is the work of Satan in this world being reported.

With this in mind, I have a suggestion for you that is 100% guaranteed to improve your "abundant life" in Christ. STOP watching and listening to any news for a month and see how your perspective changes. By doing this, you have removed a major part of Satan's influence to steal, kill, and destroy from your own life. Spend quality time with your wife and children or some friends.

You will be living the abundant life. Jesus came that you may have life and have it to its maximum. Don't compromise what Jesus has done for you.

28

ENCOURAGEMENT
WHO IS GOD?

And the Word of God says:

Acknowledge and take to heart this day that the LORD is God in heaven above and on the earth below. There is no other.

DEUTERONOMY 4:39

FROM THIS VERSE, LET'S BEGIN with the first word, "acknowledge". We acknowledge people with all kinds of general greetings. "Good morning"; "How are you doing?"; "What's happening?"; "What'cha doing?"; but, how do you acknowledge God?

It's not a bad idea to say the same general greetings to God, but I think this verse is asking for a little more in acknowledgement. It's like being in a group of people, and you see someone you know. In that case, you could make a special effort to go directly to that person and begin a conversation. Those around would conclude that you "know" that person. Don't leave God in your "general greeting" crowd. ACKNOWLEDGE Him as the LORD in heaven and on earth.

To do this, you must have the thoughts of what is in heaven and on earth. In heaven are God, Christ, Holy Spirit, all God's angels, and God's people. On earth is Satan, his demons, all the stuff the world hands us every day of our lives, AND GOD! Now, when you acknowledge God, your thoughts should be that God is over all, in control of all, plans and manages all, has His hand on all, knows all, and nothing...not anything can get past God...in heaven or on earth.

As you acknowledge God in this way and take it into your heart, you realize that God is greater than anything on this earth. Your plans, problems, and obstacles in your life change from "downers" to opportunities for God to be acknowledged. You'd better believe that you are given so many opportunities during one day to acknowledge Him as God in heaven and on earth. Do you do this? This is something that is an "inner being" thought and action. No one else would know if you are acknowledging God in your heart. Unless, the results of your acknowledgement in your innermost being bring peace, patience, wisdom, an eternal perspective, and spiritual understanding. And, that's exactly what God's Word says will happen when you acknowledge Him.

Finally, "there is no other." WOW!! As naturally rebellious toward God (and we all are!), we will look for our own way to live. We have to have things the way we think they should be in this world, and when they are not (which is all the time), we lose our joy, we become despairing, and hopeless. As this verse says, "there is no other" way other than acknowledging God as God! The LORD is God in heaven and on earth!

29

WORKS

THE WORKS OF A CHRISTIAN

And the Word of God says:

**"Be careful not to do your 'acts of righteousness'
before men, to be seen by them. If you do, you will
have no reward from your Father in heaven. So
when you give to the needy, do not announce it with
trumpets, as the hypocrites do in the synagogues
and on the streets, to be honored by men. I tell you
the truth, they have received their reward in full.
But when you give to the needy, do not let your left
hand know what your right hand is doing, so that
your giving may be in secret. Then your Father,
who sees what is done in secret, will reward you."**

MATTHEW 6:1-4

JESUS SAID THE ABOVE AS part of what is called the "Sermon on the
Mount". All my life I have heard that you cannot earn your way into
heaven…that all of my good works will not qualify me for any part of a
future eternal life with God. So, being a good Christian, I looked upon
"works" as of no value to my life. Works were meaningless to me and to
God. Man, was I wrong!! It's not works that get me to heaven – it is Christ
and Christ alone.

But what about works – "acts of righteousness" as Jesus described? Based on the above, I now believe the following about works: After a person becomes a Believer, God considers everything they do as either for Him or not for Him. If the "works" are done for Him and only for Him, then He will give rewards to the Believer in Heaven. If the "works" are not for Him, then the rewards are only those that the world provides… trophies, money, recognition, etc.

All of these things are temporary and, from an eternal perspective, meaningless. Our works as a Believer should be focused on God's kingdom. You can receive praise and blessings on this earth from others, but do not do things to gain man's approval. Just think about it! Although no one may know your "works", He does. And, your reward will come from the Creator of the Universe. WOW!

30

REST

HAVE A RELATIONSHIP OR
PRACTICE A RELIGION?

And the Word of God says:

"Come to Me, all you who labor and are heavy laden, and I will give you rest. Take My yoke upon you and learn from Me, for I am gentle and lowly in heart, and you will find rest for your souls."

MATTHEW 11:28-29

WHENEVER SCHOOL STARTS MANY PARENTS settle into a routine to ensure that their children are plugged into the right classes with the right teachers. Work continues within the family. Laundry and house cleaning has to be done. Meals need to be planned and prepared with clean up afterwards. Bills continue to arrive and need to be paid. Going to church continues as usual. Everything seems to be going pretty well. Or, is it?

How long before all of these activities become a burden? How long before one of the kids becomes sick and has to stay home from school only to pass the illness throughout the family. Everyone becomes sick and fatigue sets in to every member of the family. Projects at your work increase with no additional help. Management is demanding more output. Nerves become raw and are carried into the home after work.

The kids want the latest electronic gadget or cell phone because everyone else has one. Aging parents get sick and need some help. What was a good routine becomes a really good rut that gets deeper every day. Things seem to be going faster and faster while time can be going so slow with a sick child. And so it goes…day after day. We think to ourselves, "If only I could get away and rest for a week or a day or even a couple of hours of sleep."

The above three paragraphs describe the activity of the world. I have some news for you. All of those advertisements that say your life would be easier and you would be happier are simply lies. If anything, when you buy something, you will have to use it, or maintain it, or replace it, which will put more demands on your time. The world is not here to make your life easier…it is here to entice you to spend money that you don't have. I may be over simplifying the situation, but I think all of us have experienced the world's heavy weight on us in trying to live according to what the world promotes.

Jesus had an answer, and He gives it to you in the verses above. "Come to me!" In the paragraphs above, I know I included going to church as a worldly event in your life. That's where Jesus says the problem is. Going to church is a religious event; you are practicing a religion. Having a relationship with Christ is a spiritual event; it is the relationship that Jesus is talking about.

Other religious practices could be reading your Bible through in a year. This is a commendable activity, but by February you have either quit or it has become a ritual event that you have to do. You are "heavy laden" to make sure you get your Bible reading in for the day. Jesus encourages us to read and study our Bibles, but do it with a relationship with Him. You may sing in the choir or play a musical instrument as a religious event in your life. That's great! However, make it a spiritual event by preparing and looking for your relationship with Jesus through music and song.

You see, God sent His only Son to die on the cross and raised Him from the dead, so that Almighty God could have a relationship with you. Going to church, reading the Bible, singing a song, or whatever you do should be finding "rest for your soul". And that rest involves taking the yoke of Jesus and learning from Him.

It is a wonderful spiritual event in your life when you are reading your Bible and an hour goes by without your awareness. You are having a relationship with Him. It is a wonderful spiritual event when you see the hurt in someone else, and the Spirit shows you exactly what that person needs and you do it. You are having a relationship with Him.

I could go on and on, but developing a relationship with Jesus should be your first priority in your spiritual life. You will find rest from all the worldly stuff that you still have to do, because your spiritual eyes are set on Him. Do you really believe what He said? He will give you rest through a relationship with Him.

Section 4

Specific Topics Related to Men Chapters 31 – 40

31

ANGER

A QUICK TEMPER LITERALLY SCARES OTHERS

And the Word of God says:

Whoever is patient has great understanding, but one who is quick-tempered displays folly.

PROVERBS 14:29

"In your anger do not sin": Do not let the sun go down while you are still angry, and do not give the devil a foothold.

EPHESIANS 4:26-27

SOME SAY THAT ANGER IS the strongest of all human emotions. I believe it! I have a quick temper. I can become extremely angry within seconds over some meaningless events. At first, I thought this is how men get attention and get their way in things. But, I have found that my anger is a cover-up for not trusting God. In this chapter, I hope you can identify if you have a quick temper and become angry easy, and I hope I can adequately explain how you can take control of that anger.

In some earlier chapters, I gave examples of when I would get angry with people. On all of these occasions, God showed me how silly and ridiculous it was for me to become angry in the first place. In every situation, it was because there was a negative impact on my worldly life. I want to give you another example that produced a significant amount of embarrassment.

We were living in Florida and it had to be July or August because it was hot. I needed to work on the engine in my truck one Saturday. While I was in the middle of tuning my truck, my wife comes to me holding a bunch of pink clothing. She apologized because she had washed my five new white dress shirts to be worn to work with something red, and they had all turned pink. I cannot tell you all the things that went through my mind but some of my thoughts were "why couldn't you be more careful"; "don't you realize how much those shirts cost"; "our finances are stretched so thin and you do something like this." I know that I literally threw the wrench I was holding into the yard. I remember stomping around the truck and feeling like everything was out of control. My poor wife took the brunt of my anger and quick temper.

Years later, I look back on all of these reactions on my part and feel totally ashamed. As a man, I had lost control. I deceived myself thinking that men are suppose to get mad at things like this to be a real man. I had to show my wife that I did not like what she did, and I wanted her to feel bad about what she had done. I was so deceived.

Fortunately, I learned from these kinds of incidents God's way of handling my anger. First of all, God was and is taking care of my family and me. I don't need to yell and scream and get mad to maintain control. God showed me that He could replace those shirts at His timing, since He was able to speak the universe into existence. As for my wife, she saw me at my worst. I was not the man she married and said vows of "for better or worse, for richer or poorer". Those words mean more to me today than the day I said them to her when we were married. But in the instance involving the shirts, I damaged my relationship with her and that weighs heavy on a man when he finally realizes the futility and stupidity of showing off a quick temper or anger.

This is a bold statement, but it is Biblical: "A Christian man should never have a quick temper or become angry." I know that many of you are going to jump on that, and tell me that Jesus became righteously angry with the moneychangers in the temple. I have heard it a thousand times. I'll let you get angry the next time you have to clear the moneychangers out of your church. In other words, there is not a reason today for a Christian man to become angry to the point of damaging his relationship with those closest to him. There are no reasons!

I have talked to a lot of men with anger management problems. The key to relieving yourself of anger begins right now by declaring that God is in control, that He loves you, and, that He will protect you. A man has to see the eternal perspective of God's relationship with him, so that the anger that may come up today does not exist because of eternal thinking.

Men, I hope you work on this issue, because I believe anger scares a wife and, definitely, will scare a child. You don't need to have anger damaging your relationships with others.

32

PORNOGRAPHY
DEHUMANIZES A MAN'S
ENTIRE FAMILY

And the Word of God says:

"You have heard that it was said, 'You shall not commit adultery.' But I tell you that anyone who looks at a woman lustfully has already committed adultery with her in his heart.

MATTHEW 5:27-28

JESUS SAID THIS IN WHAT is referred to as the Sermon on the Mount that includes Matthew Chapters 5 – 7. I strongly recommend that you read those chapters several times to see what Jesus said about many topics. The two verses above describe adultery. It was common to define adultery as the physical act of sexual relations with someone other than your husband or wife. I will be speaking to men in this chapter.

It is joked that 50% of men are involved in pornography and the other 50% are in denial. I don't want this to be taken as a joke since pornography is a major problem for most men, even Christian men.

This should be a difficult chapter for every man because of the way Jesus defined adultery. Jesus took the common definition of adultery and defined what we call "pornography" today. If you think it in your mind, you have committed adultery.

It is interesting that on the Internet, Wikipedia defines pornography as follows:

> Pornography is the explicit portrayal of sexual subject matter for the purpose of sexual gratification. Pornography may use a variety of media, including books, magazines, postcards, photos, sculpture, drawing, painting, animation, sound recording, film, video, and video games. The term applies to the depiction of the act rather than the act itself.

It sounds very much like the way Jesus defined it 2,000 years ago: "the term applies to the depiction of the act rather than the act itself."

As a personal example, I bought two porno magazines and put them it the desk drawer in our home. Our children were about 5 and 7 years old at the time. Several days passed until one night after my wife and I had gone to bed, I heard her say in a hurtful voice, "I found your magazines." The room increased in temperature by 100 degrees, and I was paralyzed due to embarrassment. Those magazines had compromised my pure and innocent wife. Bile started to collect in my throat. I did not know what to say. She finally said, "Get rid of them."

I tell you this personal example, because I could see how it dehumanized, embarrassed, and cheapened the relationship between my wife and me. I look back on that incident and grew in my admiration for my wife. She handled my sin in a way that was more powerful than anything she could have done. If you are a woman reading this, I hope you can see the power of my wife's handling of this situation. She waited until the appropriate time and confronted me with the truth. She did not yell or scream or threaten. She discovered my sin and confronted me with it in love. From that point on, pornography became nauseous to me. I did not want to compromise my relationship with my wife.

Christian men: where are you on this topic of pornography? Do you participate in pornography on the Internet? Ask God to make you nauseous over pornography. Stop pursuing snatches of time to be involved with it. Pornography can easily become an addiction. It will ruin your perspective of other women. Your thoughts will be impure and full of garbage and raw sewage because of how you think of other women. Pornography is a relationship killer, especially with your wife.

I wish I could get inside your brain and every time you looked at another woman with pornography in mind, I could hit you with a 2x4 as hard as I could. But, I don't have to do that, because the Holy Spirit will do it.

Know this: I prayed as I was writing this that every man who reads this will be harshly convicted by the Holy Spirit over any impure thought. Your attitude must change toward pornography. It must look like the most disgusting and horrible thing that you could think of. If you do, you will begin to love your wife much more deeply. Remove from your home anything that hints at pornography. Put software on your personal computer that will report any access to porn sites. Finally, and this is the one that hit me the hardest, don't look at anything if you cannot allow your wife and/or daughter to be there with you. Your sexual life with your wife will be more satisfying and complete.

33

IDOLS

MAN LOVES HIS TOYS

And the Word of God says:

The idols speak deceit, diviners see visions that lie; they tell dreams that are false, they give comfort in vain. Therefore the people wander like sheep oppressed for lack of a shepherd.

ZECHARIAH 10:2

OK…OK! SO THIS IS A negative sounding verse from the Bible, but it speaks the truth, especially for the times that we are currently experiencing. When times get tough, people will try to find comfort in most anything. When times are good, they buy more idols. "Idols" are the man made objects that entice us to spend time with them thinking that comfort will come.

Idols are any "things" that we put before our relationship with others (spouse, children, family, etc., and especially God.) But "idols" rust, rot, wear out, corrode, get dirty, and become old and unattractive. Idols lie to us about providing comfort…they don't! Idols for a man are his toys. You have heard the not-so-far-from-the-truth that the only difference between men and boys are the size of their toys. Men become enamored with "toys". Some men always have to have the latest and greatest. This usually spells disaster from a financial point of view.

If you think for a moment, you know what "diviners" are...news media, stock market analysts, politicians, and even our "Uncle Jim's and Aunt Sue's" will kick in with "visions and dreams." We seek out those who will say what we want to believe thinking that this brings us comfort. But all of these things "give comfort in vain." Another way of putting this is that they give false hope. The world and the things of the world ALWAYS have and ALWAYS will give false hope. I think it's time that you reread Chapter 1 about TRUTH.

People who want to make you "feel" better have good intentions, but they deliver the wrong message. Some people may actually tell you the "truth", but they don't believe it themselves...so it gives you false hope. What is the real and true comfort and hope for people today? Jesus Christ, the Great Shepherd. We are all like sheep, distracted, gullible, easily led astray, helpless, defenseless...always looking for that "greener" pasture.

This is a major problem for men today. We wander around with a ton of weight on us, because the world has said, "Do this, buy that, and your life will be one of comfort and hope for the future." Hog Wash!!

Our comfort and hope is in Jesus Christ, who is eternal life for us. You can listen to the idols and diviners of this world, or you can focus on Him. If you think on things of this world to get comfort, then you will be in a life-long, never-ending, never-satisfying struggle with everything and everyone in your life.

What is so strange about what I am saying is that if I was 28 again and reading this, I would be blind and deaf to what it says. I would falsely believe that I have all of my toys under control. None of them control me. That's another Hog Wash! If I had a bass boat, you would not find me at home with the family very often. At one time in my life, jogging became an obsession for me. I am ashamed to say that I don't remember doing much with my family during my "jogging" days. Men, I hope you don't have toys that take you away from relationships with God, your wife, and your family.

If you focus on what God has done for you, what He is doing, and what He will do in the future, you will experience a peace that cannot be explained, comfort that gives your life meaning, and hope that encourages you daily through a relationship with Him. Try reading John 10:1–18 as a personal time of devotion this week. Ask God to show you idols in your life and get rid of them before they destroy you and your relationships.

34

HUSBANDS

LOVE YOUR WIVES – PART 1

And the Word of God says:

Submit to one another out of reverence for Christ.

Wives, submit yourselves to your own husbands as you do to the Lord. For the husband is the head of the wife as Christ is the head of the church, his body, of which he is the Savior.

EPHESIANS 5:21-23

"WIVES, SUBMIT YOURSELVES TO YOUR husbands." Other than John 3:16, there is probably not another verse that is so well known by Christians. Unfortunately, most people do not read the verse that appears before this verse: "Everyone should submit to one another." In other words, just like Christ submitted to everyone, we are to do the same. We could go round and round in circles with husbands submitting to wives and wives submitting to husbands, but God brings in a difference in the types of submission.

In the verses above, did you notice that it doesn't say, "Wives, love your husbands"? It doesn't say that. This doesn't mean that a wife is not suppose to love her husband, but God is resolving the conflict that I discussed in Chapter Five regarding the consequences of the sin of Adam and Eve.

Recall that Genesis says that the wife will want to control her husband but the husband will rule over her. This is a huge conflict in all marriages. God provides the answer to that conflict. He says for wives to "submit" or "respect" their husbands. The word submit is the word for agreeing, answering to, or responding to. Before any wives get real upset about what I said, the spiritual concept is a helper-agreeing with, following, and responding to their husband. Remember that was God's original plan for Eve as the "helper" for Adam. I want for you to hold that spiritual thought for this is what a woman does.

Now, let's include the verses that concern the husband:

> **Husbands, love your wives, just as Christ loved the church and gave himself up for her to make her holy, cleansing her by the washing with water through the word, and to present her to himself as a radiant church, without stain or wrinkle or any other blemish, but holy and blameless. In this same way, husbands ought to love their wives as their own bodies. He who loves his wife loves himself. After all, no one ever hated their own body, but they feed and care for their body, just as Christ does the church— for we are members of his body.**
>
> EPHESIANS 5:24-30

In my opinion, God places a heavier accountability for man in marriage. Man is to love his wife as Christ loves the church. How does Christ love the church? He sacrificed His life for the church – the body of Believers. Husbands are to do everything they can to love and protect their wives. They are also to help the wife grow spiritually. This can only happen if the husband has it as a purpose in his life to grow spiritually. Most Christian marriages are lop-sided and in danger today, because the husband has abdicated his spiritual responsibility for his wife and his children. The husband must be constantly growing spiritually so that he can be the spiritual leader of the home.

For example, what does Christ do with the Church? When the Church has all kinds of problems, what does Christ do? He loves it. When you go off the beaten path, what does Christ do? He loves you. He forgives you. What are husbands supposed to do from a spiritual point of view? They're supposed to so love their wives that they sacrifice themselves. The husband is not complete without his wife. He is to love, cherish, protect, provide, encourage, forgive and spend quality time with her as much as possible.

If the husband is doing that, what is the wife supposed to do? Responding to that love. Agreeing with that love. Following that love. Do you understand? The wife's actions and reactions to her husband give him the self-esteem and value that can only come from the wife. God ordained marriage in this way. It is we who have brought the world into a marriage and made it something other than God's ideal relations between man and woman.

Husbands: start working today to make your marriage stronger. You are the Leader and the Spiritual leader of the family. Don't shirk your responsibilities just because your life gets a little hard on this side of eternity. Don't abdicate your responsibilities because you allow your wife to take control. God established an order of leadership in the marriage that allows the growth of a healthy relationship between husband and wife.

Finally, husbands you will be presenting your wife to Christ as holy and unblemished. Focus on what that would take for you to do while married to your wife on this earth. This is a heavy responsibility but it is the same as Christ presenting the church to God. Your humility and submissiveness has to be effective to the point of remaining the Spiritual Leader of the home with complete support of your wife and your children. Their respect for you as the Spiritual Leader should continue to grow through the self-denial decisions that you make regarding your own life. God expects you too!

35

HUSBANDS
LOVE YOUR WIVES – PART 2

And the Word of God says:

So the Lord God caused the man to fall into a deep sleep; and while he was sleeping, he took one of the man's ribs[a] and then closed up the place with flesh. Then the Lord God made a woman from the rib he had taken out of the man, and he brought her to the man. The man said, "This is now bone of my bones and flesh of my flesh; she shall be called 'woman,' for she was taken out of man." That is why a man leaves his father and mother and is united to his wife, and they become one flesh.

GENESIS 2:21-24

I WANT TO REPEAT SOME things I said in Chapter 3. Think of the worldly definition of submission--what we have been trained and brain-washed with as far as what women are to do based on what the world says. If we consider that definition, what have we just done to God? Do you see what I'm driving at? You've got to look at the spiritual definition--what God is telling you a helper is. God said that in Psalms 30:10 and Psalm 54:4 that He was man's helper. This is the same word for woman as man's helper.

If God intended for the woman to have a certain role, a certain way of looking at things with her husband and be called "helper," what did He mean? Does that help you understand what God is as your helper? What is the wife supposed to be? The helper. The one there when you need her there. The wife is there to help her husband, just like you want God there when you're down, and things aren't going right and there are trials and tribulations. A husband needs someone to encourage him in his life and God has assigned that duty to the wife, the helper. What is the husband supposed to do? Leave the mother and father and cling to his wife.

God also says that the two shall become "one flesh?" The husband has one spiritual role in life: Take care of the helper. Love the helper. Be united with the helper. Today, tomorrow, and every day thereafter, when you're in front of the TV, and your wife needs something, what are you supposed to do? Men, as serious as I can be, you turn off that TV, and love your wife. You help her. You love her. You take care of her ahead of what you think you want. Don't say, "Well, I've worked all week. I think I've earned it."

God clearly defined marriage and the roles and responsibilities of the husband and wife. We have started "redefining" marriage to fit something that we want including same sex marriage. There is a huge spiritual reason that God defined marriage the way He did.

In Genesis God wanted to make marriage something special and unique. Do you understand why marriage is so important throughout the Bible? Because God had planned to use marriage to demonstrate the love that Christ has for the church – you and me. God did this because He uses bride and bridegroom in a marriage to illustrate His relationship with the Jews (Old Testament) first and the church (New Testament.)

Can you see how important healthy and strong marriages are to God? That's what is so sacred and precious to God about the marriage of a man and a woman. God says, "I'm going to give this to men and women. This is my concept of marriage." Now we've taken it and just turned it all upside down and made a mess of it.

Wives, submit to your husbands just as everyone is to submit to one another. Your difficulty in submitting to your husband is due to the consequences of sin discussed in Chapter 5. Wives will need to submit themselves to God and deny themselves, if they will be genuinely submissive to their husbands. Husbands, love your wives as Christ loves the church and died for it. Husbands are to completely deny themselves, if they are ever to become one with their wives.

36

FATHERS
HOW TO DISCIPLINE
YOUR CHILDREN

And the Word of God says:

People were also bringing babies to Jesus for him to place his hands on them. When the disciples saw this, they rebuked them. But Jesus called the children to him and said, "Let the little children come to me, and do not hinder them, for the kingdom of God belongs to such as these. Truly I tell you, anyone who will not receive the kingdom of God like a little child will never enter it."

LUKE 18:15-18

Whoever spares the rod hates their children, but the one who loves their children is careful to discipline them.

PROVERBS 13:24

Discipline your children, and they will give you peace; they will bring you the delights you desire.

PROVERBS 29:17

THIS CHAPTER MAY BE THE last one you read and you may throw this book away because of what I think the Bible is saying about disciplining your children. I hope you don't.

As everything else we have seen in this book, there is the worldly way of looking at discipline and then there is God's way. This discussion on disciplining children will continue into the next chapter.

There is a huge difference between punishment and discipline. I will say up-front that punishment should be seldom if ever used on a child. On the other hand, discipline should have a daily application to children. Let me explain.

Punishment is exactly that. You punish your child for something they did in the past. However, with punishment, there are no attempts on your part to teach or train your child about what they did wrong. Also, most of the time, punishment comes from your anger directed toward your child. Never, ever attempt to punish a child while you are angry. There is so much damage to relationships that eventually cannot be overcome. After finding out about a wrong that your child did, you should ensure that you are not angry. If you are, get away from the child and cool down. Otherwise, you may regret something you say or do. We are talking about little children that are much smaller than you. Your physical force driven by anger is not an acceptable way to treat a child.

You must never forget that children are very special to God. They are innocent and vulnerable. His judgment on those adults who abuse children is extremely severe.

"If anyone causes one of these little ones—those who believe in me—to stumble, it would be better for them to have a large millstone hung around their neck and to be drowned in the depths of the sea.

MATTHEW 18:6

In a way, all children belong to God and are on loan to parents. God expects parents to nurture and protect children. According to the verses above, the other expectation God has for parents is to educate them on who God is. This is probably the biggest failure of Christian fathers, because it is so easy to leave it to the wife. Christian fathers need to live a Christ-like life to be able to teach their children. You talk to your children about how God has been a part of your life. This is so important to a young child's development.

When correction is needed, a Christian father will rely on the Holy Spirit to determine the appropriate Christian discipline. Remember that discipline is teaching for the future, while punishment is giving pain for something in the past. I would suggest that the "rod" mentioned in the above verses is for punishment. But, I think the "rod" could also be several other things.

For my children, there was the rod at times, but only after discipline had occurred. For example, if there was an intentional act of disobedience, you would talk to your child about what was wrong with their behavior, and, then, the rod may be needed. Discipline always occurred.

The discipline should also fit the maturity of the child. It is hard to imagine a 3-year-old understanding punishment other than it hurt. But, using the discipline of taking away a favorite toy for a time may have much more of an impact on that child. As personal examples of discipline, my children experienced writing essay questions and answering questions from the Bible. It took time for me to do this, but I believe strongly that that was what God wanted me to do.

37

FATHERS
DO NOT EXASPERATE
YOUR CHILDREN

And the Word of God says:

In your struggle against sin, you have not yet resisted to the point of shedding your blood. And have you completely forgotten this word of encouragement that addresses you as a father addresses his son? It says, "My son, do not make light of the Lord's discipline, and do not lose heart when he rebukes you, because the Lord disciplines the one he loves, and he chastens everyone he accepts as his son." Endure hardship as discipline; God is treating you as his children. For what children are not disciplined by their father? If you are not disciplined—and everyone undergoes discipline—then you are not legitimate, not true sons and daughters at all.

HEBREWS 12:4-8

Children, obey your parents in the Lord, for this is right. "Honor your father and mother"—which is the first commandment with a promise— "so that it may go well with you and that you may enjoy long life on the earth." Fathers, do not exasperate your

> children; instead, bring them up in the training
> and instruction of the Lord.

EPHESIANS 6:1-4

I CANNOT EXPRESS STRONGLY ENOUGH how disgusted I am when a Father makes fun of one of his children. I do not know where men got the idea that ridicule would strengthen their children so that they could face the world of reality. Fathers who aggravate their children have no sensitivity to the feelings of their children. I do not believe God is pleased with such Fathers.

The verses above talk about how God disciplines His children that would include Christian men. All of us men should learn from God about how He disciplines. God makes it clear that His discipline is because He loves you. He corrects those of us who are His children. After every incident of discipline to your children, they should know that you love them and that they are your children.

The verses above also make it clear that parents are to bring their children up in the training and instruction of the Lord. Christian men: do you have family times each week where you can share what happened during the week, especially, if God was involved? At mealtime, do you spend time talking about what you have comes from God. As your children mature, do you add topics like the following?

> Finally, brothers and sisters, whatever is true,
> whatever is noble, whatever is right, whatever is
> pure, whatever is lovely, whatever is admirable—if
> anything is excellent or praiseworthy—think about
> such things.

PHILIPPIANS 4:8

Do you encourage your family to think only of the good things about other people? I overheard two four-year old girls talking about whom they liked and whom they didn't like. I can guarantee you that this type of training of these young children came from the parents.

The training and instruction that God wants parents (especially, Fathers) to use comes from the life of Christ. I strongly encourage you to make the four Gospels something that you will read and study two or three times per year. Read them to your children out of a children's Bible.

There are so many things you can do to help your children grow in the Lord. It will take patience and creativity to keep children involved, but the one key ingredient that every child will identify with is love. Love your children at all times.

38

CHURCH

IS IT A NEGOTIABLE ITEM FOR MEN?

And the Word of God says:

Guard your steps when you go to the house of God. Go near to listen rather than to offer the sacrifice of fools, who do not know that they do wrong. Do not be quick with your mouth, do not be hasty in your heart to utter anything before God. God is in heaven and you are on earth, so let your words be few.

ECCLESIASTES 5:1-2

I am positive that many of you are wondering, "Where in the world did these verses come from?" They come from the book written by the wisest man that has ever lived, King Solomon. Ecclesiastes contains the results of an "experiment" that Solomon performed on himself. He had the resources to live life any way he chose, so he decided to try different things to see what could make "man" happy. He tried wealth, possessions, honor, work, sex, food, etc. and nothing made him happy. I am sure a lot of you men would like to try the same experiments. Solomon would probably call you a fool for even trying to find happiness in the things of the world. He would violently disagree with the beer commercial that says, "It doesn't get any better than this!"

Ecclesiastes uses the word "meaningless" about 50 times to describe how everything on this earth ends in "meaninglessness". The book ends with the conclusion to "fear God and keep his commandments." The verses above come near the middle of the book. Solomon pauses in describing his various experiments to describe a person's attitude in going to the "house of God" or what we call going to "church" today.

I know the steps I went through to get to the point where if I miss church, I have missed something very important in my life. My church attendance started with "not having a choice". I had to go with my parents. By the time I was 10, church attendance became optional because both of my parents worked on Sundays. When I started working in the grocery store that my father owned, he expected me to work in the store and not go to church. My mother had other ideas, and I am glad, because that is when I accepted Jesus Christ. By the time I was going to college, I went to church so that I could take some girls, since I was the only one with a car. Unknowingly my future wife was one of those girls. By the time I was married, I had many other interests besides church. I would go to make my wife happy, but I made sure that I controlled my church attendance, because I did not want to become a fanatic.

All of the above changed when God turned me inside out when I was 30 years old. Since then, going to church is a must for me. I have to have a time of worship of God and instruction in how to live a Christian life. Church attendance is no longer drudgery or something to avoid like the plague. I have to have Jesus along with the fellowship with brothers and sisters in Christ. I hunger and thirst for God. As a man, you must have the discipline to spiritually lead your family to become a part of a local body of Believers. Theirs and your spiritual life depends on it.

When you go to church, the verses above describe God's perspective of how you should go. The verses say to guard your steps. Steps indicate a direction and a movement in that direction. This "guarding" involves your attitude in preparing to worship God. For myself, and for probably a lot of you, it's very easy to be thinking about a lot of other things when you get ready to go to church or on your way to church. You could be thinking about your job, or an incident with your spouse or children, or something that has been bugging you over the past few weeks. May I say that this is worldly thinking? It will be impossible to hear from God if your thoughts are tied up with yourself. You must prepare yourself to hear from God.

The verses go on to say that we should prepare ourselves to listen. It is interesting that the verses say that listening is God's choice for our worship of Him over sacrifices. This makes sense because frequently we treat church attendance as another check off on our list of what we think it means to be a good Christian. Guilty! But we miss God! It is imperative to hear from God first and then take action on what He reveals to us. Too often, we have already made up our minds what "church" will be like and we bring those expectations to church with us. This is all about ourselves, and what we think we should be getting out of church. God has something entirely different in mind.

Look at the other things in these verses that God says to be careful with…your mouth and your heart. Your mouth will express what it has accumulated in your heart all week. I hope you realize how spiritually dangerous this is. When we open our mouths to express our thoughts without first seeking God's guidance, nothing but trouble can result. This is why there are so many hurt feelings when people visit a church. Instead of speaking spiritual truths with other people, we want to talk about the latest on politics, sports figures, or community news that has nothing to do with the worship of God. Some people actually save up all of their stories, so that they can share them at church. People who are visiting may truly be looking for a place that puts God first and not the world. All they hear are the same things they hear at work or in their neighborhood. Our mouths should be expressing our praise and thankfulness for God…that is worship.

The verses conclude describing the frame of mind that we all should have about our approach to the worship of God. He is in heaven that is spiritual and eternal. We are on earth that is worldly and temporal. In other words, our thoughts are worthless when compared to the spiritual revelation that God desires to give each of us through His Holy Spirit. It's like we accept the garbage of this world as the truth, and God's revelation never comes into our minds.

As Spiritual Leaders of the home, men should make church attendance a priority for his family. As Believers, may we all approach God with an expectation that He will show us where we are as human beings and where He wants us as Christ-like witnesses for Him.

39

YOUR WITNESS
IN THE WORKPLACE

And the Word of God says:

But even if you should suffer for what is right, you are blessed. "Do not fear their threats; do not be frightened." But in your hearts revere Christ as Lord. Always be prepared to give an answer to everyone who asks you to give the reason for the hope that you have. But do this with gentleness and respect, keeping a clear conscience, so that those who speak maliciously against your good behavior in Christ may be ashamed of their slander.

1 PETER 3:14-16

THIS IS A VOLATILE TOPIC, because the workplace is viewed as a place where no religious activities can occur. In all of my years of working, I never had a problem with that, and I was still able to witness for the Lord. I never initiated a conversation about God, but plenty of people wanted to talk to me about God, and I did.

I want to give you some of the actual events that I became involved with in the workplace.

Be patient with sinners: An employee of the company that I was providing consulting support to came to me one day and asked if we could eat lunch together. Of course! He and I started at least weekly if not more than two or three times per week eating lunch together. He asked me if I was a Christian, and I said yes. After a couple of months, he began to tell me about how he was going to divorce his wife. He also told me he was involved with another woman.

I did not judge him for this unless he asked my opinion. He also was having troubles with two teen-age daughters and was in financial debt. After two years of meeting and talking, he came to the realization that he was the one causing all of the problems. Soon afterwards, he left the company. A few months went by when he called me and asked me to come to his church, because he had accepted Jesus Christ as Lord and Savior, and he wanted me to be their for his baptism. He also told me that he and his ex-wife had been dating and were married again. Praise God for a life that changed even though it took a long time.

Deny myself or deny the Lord: This event occurred when my supervisor and his manager called me into the manager's office to have a "talk". They placed a chair in the middle of the room and proceeded to tell me that I was doing outstanding work. I was performing far beyond anything that they had imagined. For that reason, they wanted to put me on the "fast-track" within the company, so that promotions would occur on a regular basis with increased responsibility. At first, my head got bigger because of their praise. It made me feel really good to have my management talk to me about this. I also thought that this is the kind of thing that every employee dreams about.

Finally, after almost 30 minutes of them talking about the options I had, it was my turn to answer the question, "What would you like to be doing in the company in 5, 10, 15, and 20 years?" The first thing that hit me was the Holy Spirit leading me to say that God would take care of me. For the next 30 minutes, I was waging a spiritual battle within myself, because I could see that this event was an opportunity to witness for God.

The only problem was the flesh in me was rearing its ugly head and giving me a hard time. It was clearly a decision between the flesh and God. I finally told management that I appreciated their encouragement and their fantastic offer to take care of me, but I told them that God would take care of me. I would not have to plan anything. During those last 30 minutes, management tried to get a different answer from me, because they basically ignored my witness for God.

I wonder where he is now: This is a story that is difficult for me to tell. In an earlier chapter, I described a man who was known by everyone in the company as the "manager from a different planet". As you may recall I described him as arrogant, egotistical, narcissistic, sacrilegious, an atheist, and the list could go on. For the first six months that I worked with him, I could not wait for God to get me away from him. However, God led me to read Psalms and Proverbs every month that I was working for him.

For some reason that I cannot explain, he decided that he wanted to be with me and not other people. We had lunch together almost everyday. When I would silently bless my food, he would reach over and shake my plate or rattle my silverware or throw my napkin in the floor. I really did not want to be with this person. Then, God got a hold of me through the reading of His Word, and showed me that I was the only living being that this man would ever listen to about the story of Jesus Christ. When God convicted my heart of that, that manager could do anything and say anything he wanted to, but he was not going to have an impact on me. And he didn't. At one of our lunches, he asked me to go by the bank with him. He forced me to go with him to the teller, so that I would see four $5,000 CDs that he was renewing. He said in a very condescending manner that he would be independently wealthy when he was 54 years old.

During the next few years, I would tell him about God and Jesus Christ. I actually gave him a Bible. He started reading it and asking me questions until he got to the point in Genesis when people lived for 700 years. To my knowledge, he never read that Bible again. We both changed jobs and moved to different cities and tried to stay in touch. One day I received a call from him telling me that they had found cancer in his body and gave him three months to live. He asked me to come to Florida and talk with him again about God. We met in a bar (of course for him), and I shared the good news of Jesus Christ with him. We ate lunch and I prayed for his situation with his approval. We said our goodbyes and I returned to New York.

In less than two months, a common friend of ours called me to tell me he had died. He was 54 years old. I don't know if he is in heaven. But, I can tell you that he became a very close friend of mine. God showed me more about having strong convictions about my belief through this man than any other man. I can't wait to get to heaven and ask for him.

You can witness at your workplace, but as the verses above say, witness with gentleness and respect. People in your workplace will become aware of your beliefs and your convictions. Live your life for God where you work. You will be surprised at what God will do.

40

ACCOUNTABILITY
YOU WILL BE HELD ACCOUNTABLE

And the Word of God says:

As iron sharpens iron, so one person sharpens another.

PROVERBS 27:17

I WOULD NOT BE THE Christian man I am today if it were not for several brothers in Christ who met with me on a regular basis. It started in Florida when the Associate Pastor asked if I would meet with him at his house every Tuesday at 5:30AM. I agreed and for the next four years we met weekly. I'll never forget how he helped me get through so many Christian topics during that time.

Whenever my family moved, I sought out men who would meet with me on a weekly basis. I asked them to hold me accountable for everything that I have discussed in this book. Looking back on the past 35 years of accountability, I would not be who I am today.

Men: each one of you needs an accountability partner to hold you accountable. Most of you know why. We, men, tend to take things to extreme and allow our pride to enslave us to a life that is ungodly. An accountability partner will not let that happen. When you have to meet with another man each week, you soon find that you cannot hide anything. At the same time, knowing that you will be meeting with that person empowers you to overcome the flesh in you and grow spiritually.

I have one friend who calls me every Thursday night from New York. While we lived in New York, he and I met for several years and became accountable to one another. He has been calling for 14 years. It means so much to me for him to hear what I am going through, and for me to hear how his family is doing. We always pray for one another and our families. It is priceless, and I praise God for that kind of relationship.

I don't understand how a Christian man can get through this world without this kind of accountability. I want to encourage you to ask the Holy Spirit to select another Christian man as an accountability partner. You'll never regret it!

Section 5

Future Expectations
Chapters 41 – 52

41

EXPECTATIONS
WHAT DOES GOD WANT OF YOU?

And the Word of God says:

But Samuel replied: "Does the Lord delight in burnt offerings and sacrifices as much as in obeying the Lord? To obey is better than sacrifice, and to heed is better than the fat of rams. For rebellion is like the sin of divination, and arrogance like the evil of idolatry. Because you have rejected the word of the Lord, he has rejected you as king."

1 SAMUEL 15:22-23

WHAT DOES GOD WANT OF you? To answer this question, remember that He is your Creator and Sustainer...He is all-powerful and all knowing...He loves you and forgives you of all of your sins through Christ. In other words, think first of what God has done so that you can have a living and vibrant relationship with Him. He wants a relationship with you so much that He gave Himself. So, what does God want of you?

Going to church, studying your Bible, praying for your needs, asking forgiveness for sins? May I say "NO"! God wants "YOU"...your heart, mind, and soul focused on Him. In the verses above, Samuel was talking to the first king of Israel, Saul. Saul blew it with his relationship with God, because Saul focused everything on how he felt, and what he thought, and what he decided – just like most men today. When Saul had problems, he wanted to reason with God about his decisions. God was not part of Saul's life where it made a difference.

How about you? Are you going through life trying to take care of yourself (including your relationship with God?)? Are you going through the motions with no thoughts about who God is and what He has done in your life? May I say that, according to the verses above, you are being disobedient to God, and, in some aspects of your life, God will say "NO"? You leave Him no choice. When you are in church, when you are reading the Bible, when you are praying...think, ponder, meditate on God and not yourself. You will have life and have it more abundantly.

42

YOUR LIFE
GOD HAS A PLAN

And the Word of God says:

"For I know the plans I have for you," declares the Lord, "plans to prosper you and not to harm you, plans to give you hope and a future."

JEREMIAH 29:11

I'LL BET EVERY MAN LOVES the verse above. It sounds almost too good to be true. This verse gives such a peace about the life of a person. Just think that God, who created everything, has plans for you! I know personally that we would like to believe that we are in control of our own destiny. Oh, we try to figure out God's will for our lives, but usually we have already made up our minds, and all we want is a rubber stamp of approval from God. God's plans for your life are to bring you to a point of accepting Him and to be a witness to others for Him.

God's ultimate desire is that every person will believe in Him…that everyone chooses Jesus Christ as their Savior and Lord. The plan God has for your life is to satisfy that desire. However, God gave us a free will to reject Him. I say it this way, because I believe that everyone who is born has his or her name written in the Book of Life. This is the book that God looks at to determine who will live with Him in heaven. The names of all babies and children are in that book.

What happens during a person's life is that God has planned events that will cause that person to think of God. God will repeatedly reveal Himself to each and every person. These are some of the plans that God has for everyone. Eventually, each person will accept or reject God's revelation. If they consciously and intentionally reject God's revelation, then, eventually, God removes their name from the Book of Life. Therefore, some of God's plans are all about you having God reveal Himself to you in a way that is special and unique for you.

When you reach the point of accepting God's revelations and become a Believer, God has some new and different plans for your life. These plans are to position your life in such a way that you will become more Christ-like in your attitudes and behavior. God wants this because your life becomes a living testimony for Him. Others will see Christ in you and want to know more about God.

The verse above is exciting, because God says that He has plans to prosper you. We all like to prosper! I don't think that God means wealth from a world's point of view. I think God is saying that the life you have knowing Him will be full and abundant from a spiritual perspective. Your life will definitely be prosperous when you consider that you are a co-heir with Christ in God's Kingdom. He also says that He has plans not to harm you. This involves God's judgment of our sins. Christ paid the price for our sins on the cross. Therefore, those of us who trust in the work of Christ will not suffer separation from God because of our sins.

God also has plans to give us a hope and a future. As already mentioned above, we will be co-heirs with Christ. We will also live an eternal life with God. God's original plan for us as human beings was to have an eternal relationship with Him. Our sins destroy that relationship. Because of His work to restore a right relationship with us, we will live with Him eternally. At some time in the future, our bodies will be resurrected and changed into a glorified body that will never grow old and die. WOW!!

So, you can create your own plans for your life without God and, I believe, they will fail. You may reach a worldly goal through your plans, but you will not have the basis for a truly contented life. Your life will be purposeless and hopeless. Only through the TRUTH about life will a person understand the true meaning of life. God has plans for you to discover that true meaning of life. When you do discover it, you'll wonder why you waited so long.

43

YOUR LIFE
JUST THE WAY YOU ARE

And the Word of God says:

And so we know and rely on the love God has for us. God is love. Whoever lives in love lives in God, and God in him. In this way, love is made complete among us so that we will have confidence on the day of judgment, because in this world we are like him. There is no fear in love. But perfect love drives out fear, because fear has to do with punishment. The one who fears is not made perfect in love.

1 JOHN 4:16-18

WHEN I WAS WRITING THIS, I could not help but think of how a "man" thinks of the word "love." My first thought was soft, mushy, ooey-gooey, romantic stuff. You know…the same reaction men have when watching a chick flick. There's something about being "soft" that repels a man. As I continue to learn more about God, the more, as a man, I discover how woefully lacking I am in the reality of God's love. Because, you see, God is everything you can imagine about the word "love", because He is LOVE. God loves you unconditionally. I'm not so sure that anyone on this earth can love someone else unconditionally in the same the way that God loves you.

I don't know about you, but when things are bad in my life, it is reassuring to know that the Creator of the Universe really cares for me. WOW!! It doesn't matter to Him if you are rich or poor. It doesn't matter to Him if you have a high paying job or you just lost your job. It doesn't matter to Him if you can run a marathon or barely walk across the room. It even doesn't matter to Him if you believe in Him or not... He still loves you!

That's pretty hard to find in the world today. But, there's more!! His kind of love removes all fear. There are lots of things that are scaring people today. The economy, terrorism, divorces, raising children, jobs, health, and the list goes on and on. You think that's why God puts such an emphasis on His kind of love and not ours? Ours is here today if we feel like it, and gone tomorrow if we feel like it. Most, if not all, of our love is conditional, because we were raised that way. His love is eternal and unconditional. When things are getting tight and tough for you, focus on how God loves you just the way you are. Let me repeat that, "JUST THE WAY YOU ARE!"

44

YOUR LIFE
HOW TO GROW
SPIRITUALLY? – PART 1

And the Word of God says:

**But grow in the GRACE and KNOWLEDGE of our
Lord and Savior Jesus Christ.**

2 PETER 3:18

A 2009 SURVEY SAYS THAT ONLY ONE out of FIVE Christians has any interest in spiritual growth. HUH??? That's only 20%...what about the other 80%? Does that statistic fit people like you or your family? It is difficult for me to accept that there are that many Believers who do not even think about growing spiritually. Until, that is, I thought about my own life.

At the age of 30, I considered that life was all about me and I, frankly, was miserable...extremely miserable...and I made everyone around me miserable (just ask my wife.) I had been a Believer for 18 years...I was one of the FOUR out of FIVE! ...One of the 80% and did not know it!! God intervened and showed me that His way was the TRUE WAY to live a life. But I was woefully inadequate to learn about a new way of living.

I did not know the Bible or things of the church. I was constantly intimidated by the "maturity" of other believers. I did not know how to "grow" spiritually. With this in mind, I want to help you if you have decided to grow in Christ. The scriptural basis for this growth is 2 Peter 3:18 – "But grow in the GRACE and KNOWLEDGE of our Lord and Savior Jesus Christ."

Grow in Knowledge

Let me make sure you know what kind of knowledge this is. This is not head knowledge. You don't take an IQ test to see if you are spiritually knowledgeable. You also don't ask if you finished high school or if you have two or three PhDs. This kind of knowledge is where you know someone else so well that you can tell the way they think and act. You have become so familiar with them that you know how they will react in certain situations. Usually, this is your spouse and/or your children. However, I believe you should know God better than anyone else in this world.

How do you get to know your wife or your children? You could go to the library and check out a book that someone has written on your family. I don't think most families have books written about them, unless they are really famous, and they are usually dead. You could put your family in a laboratory and observe them for many years. I don't think that's feasible, and, besides, the results would be worthless, because you are not interacting with them. You could let others tell you about them, but that's not the same as getting to "know" them. You would have some facts about them and that's about all.

So, how do you get to know someone in a way that you "know" that person? First of all, you spend a lot of time with them. You listen to them talk about things, and they listen to you. There is an interaction that occurs when you are trying to understand what they are saying. You also get to know them when you are involved with the same activities as they are. Over time, you will learn their behavior, their personality, and what makes them tick. Your "knowledge" of them will grow day by day. You'll get to know them better than anyone else in the world.

God wants you to know Him in this way, so that you will know who He is and His will for your life. Yet, how do Christians increase their knowledge of God? First of all, they read their Bible. And, when they read their Bible their goal should be to get to know God and not just to become a better Christian. I know a lot of people who read the Bible through in a year with no new knowledge of God. Why? Because they had a goal to read the Bible through in a year, and they did it.

Do you see how you can read the Bible for the wrong reason? The purpose of reading and studying the Bible is to get to know God? Who is He? How does He act and react in situations? What is He trying to tell you about Himself? A Believer needs to interact with God in His Word. You interact when there is something you don't understand, and you ask the Holy Spirit to help you understand it. As a matter of fact, before you open your Bible, you should ask the Holy Spirit to show you things about God. And, He will! One secret I can give you now about knowing God is to get to know Christ. Jesus said if you have seen Him then you have seen God. Get to know Jesus, and you'll get to know God.

Begin to be intentional about your spiritual growth by purposefully getting to know Jesus Christ. Read your Bible for the right reason: to get to know God and His Son, Jesus Christ. May I suggest you buy a Bible that you are willing to write in? I always buy the $4.95 small Bible that has the New Testament and the Psalms and Proverbs from the Old Testament. There are several things you can do. Read the gospels with a highlighter and highlight only the words of Christ. Read the gospels again and highlight only the questions of Christ. Read the gospels again highlighting only the things that people said to Christ. Read the Psalms and Proverbs highlighting verses that appeal to you. I could go on with ways to get to know God through His Word. Think of some ways yourself. The results will be an increased knowledge of God and Christ. Go and get that Bible today and start highlighting today.

Become one of the ONE out of FIVE!

45

Your Life
How to Grow
Spiritually? – Part 2

And the Word of God says:

But grow in the GRACE and KNOWLEDGE of our Lord and Savior Jesus Christ.

2 Peter 3:18

A s you will recall from the last chapter, I discussed with you the need for spiritual growth of Christians. No one seems to disagree that we do not have a spiritually mature group of Believers in our churches. The above verse seems to me a key to growing spiritually, but Christians are not putting any time into the two aspects of spiritual growth: knowledge and grace. We seem to be content with what the world has to offer, and we do not stretch ourselves to be more for God. We also lack the discipline to make the hard decisions to grow spiritually. It is so easy to lay back and muddle through this world on the world's terms. It is also very depressing.

Let me remind you that Satan has created the philosophies of this world to cause you to be distracted, confused, disheartened, and to just plain forget God while living life on this earth. God's ideal has a much different application. He desires a working, loving, daily, and personal relationship with you. But, you have to work at it! And, that's what Part 1 and this chapter (Part 2) is all about.

Part 1 was to grow in KNOWLEDGE of our Lord and Savior Jesus Christ. I mentioned some of the practical ways to get to know Him, and I hope you tried some of those. I have repeatedly completed them several times and find out something different every time. Remember to get your highlighter and DO IT!

This second part is the more difficult to discuss, because I believe most Christians, if asked by a non-believer, would struggle to adequately explain what "grace" is. You have heard hundreds of sermons and Bible Study classes focused on this one word grace, but I don't believe we continually work at grasping what God intended when He showed grace to all mankind on the cross of Christ. I don't expect to enlighten you any more on its meaning, but I'll try. Some new ideas about grace may come in on the discussion on practical application.

Grow in Grace

The simplest definition is "to give someone else something of value, free when they did not deserve it." You can reword this from a God point of view to say John 3:16, "For God so loved the world that He gave His only begotten Son that whoever believes in Him will have everlasting life." If anything comes of this discussion, I hope it would be a greater appreciation for God's grace. It is only a deep understanding of God's grace that separates us (or makes us holy) before the non-believers of this world.

Satan has attempted to dilute the concept of "grace". He has done this with what jumps in our minds when we hear the word grace: "A beautiful lady appearing to walk on air across a room with her dress flowing behind her." We refer to her as graceful or full of grace. Children grow up with the idea that grace is something you say before you can eat. In sports, grace is called true sportsmanship. Can you see why our minds have been trained to focus on other things rather than the meaning of Christ dying on the cross?

This is what I am asking you to do as you read this chapter. Search your mind deeply right now and see what your mind thinks about grace. Most of us will have visions other than the meaning of the cross of Christ. God must cry, like He did over Jerusalem, over our lack of understanding of His grace.

Grace is God's unmerited favor for sinful man. To truly understand grace, we must look at ourselves as low-down, no-good-for-nothing, black-hearted, the worse of the worst sinners that ever existed. I know you are thinking of Hitler, or Idi Amin, or Stalin, or any other world figure that has to be more of a sinner than you. You can't do that! You are just as bad a sinner as the worst of all the sinners that ever lived. If you don't get this into your head, you will never understand and appreciate God's concept of "grace". Can you see the opposite of Satan's concept and God's concept? This truth is absolutely a required part of grace. You and I, your mother and your father, your children, and all your relatives and friends are alienated from God due to our sin.

What we deserve from the sins for each of us is judgment: God's judgment. We deserve to be thrown into the Lake of Fire (see Revelation 19) by God as punishment for our sins. We deserve to be totally and everlastingly through all eternity separated from God and what we envision as heaven. We deserve to feel the sensation of burning without ever burning up because of our sins. We deserve to live in darkness where we can see nothing, and it will last for an eternity. We will never see our loved ones who accepted Christ. Our thoughts will torment us forever and ever with "where's God?" and, "where is my wife," and "where are my children," and, "where are my grandchildren?" These will be our thoughts over and over and over without end.

Hopelessness will never be as real as it will be in the Lake of Fire. We think to ourselves, "why couldn't all of my good deeds and money given to the church and charities be enough to at least temporarily end this misery for a few moments…just a few moments?" But, for eternity, our torturous condition goes on and on. Can you see what God's judgment of sin without the blood of Christ does to people in eternity? This concept of our sin is a huge part of grace. Do you think Satan would want these ideas to be in your head? They are not nice. So, as human beings, we naturally do things to remove ourselves from thinking of such awful thoughts. But, for God, this is reality in eternity. God hates sin, and we are covered with sin.

The other aspect of grace that we must get into our hard-hearted life is that God loves. He loves so much that He gave His most treasured possession…Himself in the human form of Jesus Christ. Although the nails of the cross, the beatings, the blood, the disrespect, and more was placed upon Jesus, God said that this must happen for mankind to have a relationship with a holy God. There was no other way. From Genesis 3 and throughout the Bible, there is no forgiveness of sins except through the taking of life and spilling of blood. Even while on the cross, grace revealed itself when Jesus said, "Father, forgive them, for they do not know what they do!"

You see, I don't think we think about our sins and God's love to the depth of our innermost being, to appreciate what God's grace is and what it means to a non-believer. Satan has ruined grace, and he continues to distract us from our sin and God's love. Start today to spend some time recognizing what a terrible sinner you are. Don't dwell on how bad someone else is. It has to be personal! And more personal! And even more personal! Get this idea of being a sinner is your natural condition. There is nothing you can do to change it. Nothing!

Let me give you some practical applications for growing in grace. Ask the Holy Spirit to show you someone who is not your favorite person. Identify something of value that you can give them, or, listen to this carefully, something you can DO for them. Consider again what God did for you, and that is getting closer to God's grace than just giving them something. And, you know the next step – DO IT!

Another suggestion is to put others first in everything. I love to stand back and watch "Christians" position themselves to be first in line after "grace" is said at a Christian fellowship as opposed to allowing guests to go first. There are so many simple ways to show grace as your unmerited favor for sinful man. Do you get it yet? I hope so. If not, try rereading this chapter several times. Try to get yourself out of being a sinner. Don't think about the unconditional love that God has for you. You don't do a thing to receive this kind of love.

Practice this kind of love on others and watch the Holy Spirit take over and spiritual changes occur. That's why Jesus Christ died on the cross – his expression of grace.

46

GOD

WOULD YOU JUDGE AND

CONDEMN GOD?

And the Word of God says:

"Would you discredit my justice? Would you condemn me to justify yourself?

JOB 40:8

THIS IS A TOUGH VERSE for anyone who has gone through a crisis in their life, which I think would include all of us. When bad things happen to us, the world has trained us to blame God. It's almost impossible to see this blaming God in ourselves, because our flesh deceives us. But, look and listen carefully to others who are going through some tough times and you will hear for yourself.

For example, one question that is asked about God when bad things happen to innocent people is "why did He allow evil?" Underlying this question is the "hopeful existence" of an easy life with no responsibility and no hard times. The answer is simple: for God to grant us freedom of choice, He had to give us a choice...a decision between good and evil. Without this choice, we would be just like any other animal. We would be robots responding to a dictator God with no choices between good and evil. The flesh in us becomes extremely aggressive by thinking that life on this earth would be a lot better if God would take away the evil ones.

Well, this raises another question, "who is evil?" Guess what? You are! I am! Everyone is! That's why Christ gave himself for us.

God is either God or he is something that you have created in your mind to justify your own selfish way of living. And, the verse above says that when life throws something at us that is not under our controlled way of living, we blame God for not being in control and not taking care of little old me! Hogwash! (Note: that's Latin for "that's just a bunch of junk!")

Would you judge and condemn God, because your life is hard? Would you judge and condemn God, because things haven't worked out the way you planned? Would you judge and condemn God, because every time one problem gets resolved, two more pop up? This is the world and you are living your Christian life in this world. God is your only hope for relief from this world.

As for now, God has granted Satan dominion over this world due to our sin. But, Jesus has conquered all that Satan could throw at Him while Jesus lived on this earth. When Jesus was raised from the dead, he overcame the Number One fear tactic used by Satan…death.

For Christians, death is a "going to sleep" to be raised with a new spiritual body that will live with God for an eternity. At the end times, Satan will be bound up and thrown into eternal separation from God and you and me. Praise the Lord for the coming new heaven and new earth. You will not want to miss it!

So, the next time you want to blame God for something, pause and remember that He is the only Way, the only Truth, and the only Life to live in this world. Please do not condemn God just because you think you have the right to know everything. That kind of thinking is the epitome of arrogance. Instead, humble yourself before Him recognizing that you are not worthy of anything, and He is worthy of everything.

47

YOUR LIFE
GIVE CAREFUL THOUGHT
TO YOUR WAYS

And the Word of God says:

Now this is what the LORD Almighty says: "Give careful thought to your ways. You have planted much, but have harvested little. You eat, but never have enough. You drink, but never have your fill. You put on clothes, but are not warm. You earn wages, only to put them in a purse with holes in it." This is what the LORD Almighty says: "Give careful thought to your ways.

HAGGAI 1:5-7

T HESE ARE FANTASTIC VERSES TO compare what it means to think "spiritually" and what it means to think "worldly". God tells us to "give careful thought to your ways."

Most of us do a lot of thinking when we go about doing things. A lot of these thoughts are not necessarily healthy. There is not much we do as human beings that is not preceded by what we think about something, before we do that something. I don't know if that sentence makes sense but I think it does. What I'm trying to say is that if someone asks us to do something, there is a hesitation before we tell the person that we will do what they ask. Now, there can be all kinds of thoughts going through a person's head when this happens. Thoughts like, "why don't they do it themselves?" or, "why are you asking me?" or, "do I have time to do this?" or, "why don't you ask someone else?"

The thoughts we have before we take action come from the way we look at the world. And, the way we look at the world comes from pieces in all of our past experiences. I think all of you would agree that from the world's perspective, a person should be all about themselves. This world view would have a set of values that originate and end with each person. Each person decides what is good/bad, healthy/unhealthy, beneficial/unprofitable, and, especially, what is right/wrong. The verses above describe a person who has this kind of selfish world view. The ultimate end of a selfish life lived only for that person is emptiness. That person may have a lot of things during their life but all of their accumulated things do not satisfy the real, genuine, and true need of human beings – relationships.

The verses above say that "you planted much, but harvested little." This is like working for a company for the goal of earning a lot of money, so that you won't have financial problems. There are way too many life testimonies of people who have placed their priority on their job for their whole life and end up with that company saying, "you've been one of the hardest working employees we've ever had, but now we don't need you." You planted a lot, but end up with nothing. Your goal should have been to your wife and children. You can have that goal and still give your best to a company. The problem is not who you worked for, it's what you set as your goal – to make money.

This same "world view" is seen in the other parts of the verses above. An unrealistic value placed on food, drink, and clothes can set you up for a world view of selfishness. I know you may be wondering about food and drink but unless, as a Believer, you think that God provides all that you need, you will build a structure of belief in your life that says, "look what I've got!" It is so much easier to become a part of this kind of world view, because that's all we see on TV, in movies, in our neighbors and, even in our families. Clothes have become ridiculous. The price we pay for someone to wash jeans until they are faded and then tear holes in those same jeans is about as far away as you can get from God calling you a good steward of the resources He has given you. We need to give careful thought to our ways!

Finally, the ending of the verses above include what we do with money. There is nothing wrong with money from the Bible's point of view. God has provided for everyone who belongs to Him. Where Christians get into trouble with money is when we see it as a way to buy our happiness, or to hoard the money for future use for ourselves (which is usually squandered by our children or grandchildren, or even our government.)

As Believers, we also use money to purchase our social standing so that others can see that we have the same or more than they do; in other words, "look at my success." All of this is a "rat race" to look better than the next person. The problem is everyone else has the same philosophy of living; so, the measure of success escalates and escalates…you'll never reach that goal! What a waste of God's resource! You will agree when I say that it looks like the more money someone makes, the more holes they find in their pockets, and the more money they must make. This never ends when your goal for money is set on the things of this world. God says to "give careful thought to your ways!"

God is asking you in these verses to seriously consider what your thoughts are on living life on this earth. Is it all about you? Or, is it all about living a life for Him? Most of you are now thinking of ways to justify or rationalize what you have. Don't! If your use of God's resources has been wasted on you, ask God to forgive you, know that He has forgiven you, and start giving careful thoughts to your life. Your life goal should be to bring glory to God! You can't do that when you are juggling all the things in this world that would seem to provide a happy life. The world is not here to provide you a happy life. It is here to take from you everything that will satisfy the deepest needs in your life. God has provided everything you need to have all of those deepest needs met by loving Him and serving others.

48

ETERNITY
YOU HAVE TO DECIDE
THERE IS NO GOD

And the Word of God says:

"He has made everything beautiful in its time. He has also set eternity in the hearts of men; yet they cannot fathom what God has done from beginning to end."

ECCLESIASTES 3:11

WOW!! THIS IS AN UNBELIEVABLE statement about God. He has made everything and everything will be beautiful in its time. For people, He has created a new spiritual being in each Believer that will be made "like Him" in heaven. Instead of climbing Mt Everest, a Believer will descend to the top of Mt. Everest. For the earth, He will, one day, make a new earth that will be unbelievably beautiful. Think of a grander Grand Canyon or a larger Niagara Falls. Can you imagine this?

But even more amazing about the above verse is that He has put the reality of "eternity" into everyone. I take this to mean that every single living human being has inside of them the yearning and potential to know God. It takes a decision by a person NOT to believe there is a God. It's like what God put into migrating birds and animals. Somehow, by God's design, these birds and animals have an internal clock and GPS system that motivates them to move at a precise time of the year and to a particular location that may be thousands of miles away. WOW!!!

But, when God planted the idea of Him inside of us, unlike the migrating birds and animals, He gave man the opportunity to decide to migrate toward Him or away from Him. And, the further people remove God from their lives the more they cannot "fathom" that there is a God. And, just like any bird or animal that does not migrate will be in trouble, a person will face all kinds of troubles in living a life without God.

Do you live each day in the amazing wonderment of what God has done and will do? Such a perspective will definitely change the way you live your life. Migrate toward the One that put eternity into your heart!

49

GOD

YOU ARE MISSING A LOT
WITHOUT HIM IN YOUR LIFE!

And the Word of God says:

I meditate on your precepts and consider your ways. I delight in your decrees; I will not neglect your word.

PSALM 119:15-16

PSALM 119 IS THE LONGEST chapter in the Bible. It takes a few days to read all of it; at least, it does for me. The primary purpose of Psalm 119 is to talk about your relationship with God by thinking about His nature. This is done through the Bible itself. Reading and studying the Bible are necessary for you to learn more about God. You will learn about what He thinks about things. You will learn about His value system; about His ethics; the way He goes about judging. It's one thing to "talk" about God's Word with others; it's another thing to read it for yourself.

Don't give me that "I don't understand what it is saying!" Then, read and study the parts you do understand and other parts of the Bible will start to be revealed to you by the Holy Spirit. For example, the birth of Christ in Luke, Chapters 1 & 2 is not that difficult, as most children know the story. But, in that story is one of the most powerful and shortest verses about God. **For no word from God will ever fail** (Luke 1:37). If, however, you, as a Christian, do not take the time to read and study the Bible, how will you ever know more about God and His extreme desire to have a personal relationship with you?

The verses above are an encouragement for you to start reading and studying today. There are four key phrases: (1) meditate on your precepts; (2) consider your ways; (3) delight in your decrees; and, (4) not neglect your word. I would like to discuss each one to help you read and study His Word:

1. **Meditate on your precepts:** Meditate is something everyone does but is not aware of it. Meditation as a religious act has been heavily applied to Eastern religions. This has kept many Christians from meditating. However, meditation is something that God clearly desires of you, as a Christian. Meditation is NOT an emptying of your mind but rather an intense focus on something. In the verse above, the focus is to be on God's precepts. A precept is a "commandment" usually regarding moral conduct. As soon as I say "moral conduct," we Christian men have a lot of work to do. When you meditate on God's precepts, you are focusing on why God has His commandments and what they have to do with who He is. He is the protector of the weak, helpless, orphans, widows, etc. Do you meditate on those same people? Do you see them in your neighborhoods, communities, or in the world? Just this meditation alone speaks volumes about what this world would be like without God.

2. **Consider your ways:** I love the word "consider." It lets me look at something from several different perspectives to arrive at a conclusion. In this case, we have to consider God's ways. When Jesus was confronted with the prostitute caught in the act, consider how He redirected the attention of her accusers to themselves. Similar to this situation is when someone is speaking badly about someone else, and there is no one there to protect that person's reputation. Would God do it? This is "considering His ways." When you consider His ways, you will be better prepared to act Christ-like in a situation that God has prepared you for.

3. **Delight in your decrees:** You could almost call this an oxymoron. Delight is a sign of being pleased, while decrees refer to the established laws of God. One dictionary defined decrees as "God's eternal, unchangeable, holy, wise, and sovereign purpose, comprehending at once all things that ever were or will be in

their causes." I like that definition! When I read a magazine that discusses evolution, life on other planets, the vastness of millions of universes, or any other science article, it is very hard not to "delight in God's decrees." An example of this is when the article is speaking of the mathematical preciseness of the planet earth to sustain life. Another example is the theory of the God-particle that existed before the Big Bang. I don't look on these theories as man's way of explaining the laws of the universe but as God's decrees. It is astounding that there is a God who has decreed all that we sense, plus what we don't sense, and He desires a personal relationship with me. Wow!

4. **Not neglect your word:** If we neglect God's word, consider the previous three things that you would have missed. How can you? God has created something that is like nothing little, finite man could have envisioned. This fact drives me to read and study His Word. And, the more I do, the more I find the Truth about life that I can't find in any science or psychology book. For someone to live his or her life without God is depressing. For a Christian to live their life without reading and studying God's Word is despairing. A Christian misses the best of their life when they do not spend time in the Bible. I have spent 35 of my 65 years in the Bible and can read any atheistic book, science book, etc. and find God all over the place.

I wish and pray the same for you. Your life will never be the same.

50

EXPECTATIONS
WHAT GOD EXPECTS OF YOU

And the Word of God says:

"He has showed you, O man, what is good. And what does the Lord require of you? To act justly and to love mercy and to walk humbly with your God?"

MICAH 6:8

THIS VERSE ABSOLUTELY SURPRISED ME the first time I read it. If you ever wanted the Bible to tell you what God wants you to do, well, this it. God has shown you what is good. You can't say that if God would only show you something, you would do it. NO! He has shown you what is good.

To act justly. In every situation, we should try to see things from God's perspective. His criterion for "justice" is eternal. We sometimes want to pronounce judgment before considering the eternal significance of our decision on the lives of others.

To love mercy. This is easy for those who are in need...Yes! But, what about those who deserve our anger, but we show them mercy; just like God is showing to you because of Jesus.

To walk humbly with your God. As a constant reminder, I consider myself as a human being with a severe flaw...I am a sinner...I disobey God. (That could get a person depressed.) But, because of Jesus Christ, I will one day walk with God as a child of His. I do not know another thought that I could possibly think of that will keep me humble. It's when I forget God that pride comes storming into my life. And even then, God's forgiveness is complete, unconditional, and FREE! I am humbled by His constant and unfailing love for me. How about you?

51

Your Life
Time for a Revival

And the Word of God says:

"Therefore tell the people: This is what the Lord Almighty says: 'Return to me,' declares the Lord Almighty, 'and I will return to you,' says the Lord Almighty."

ZECHARIAH 1:3

DO YOU FEEL AS THOUGH God is some where out in space…not involved with your life? The things that happen to you are because of luck or fate? When the majority of your thinking is on this world, you build a "life philosophy" based on this world. Return means to go or come back. Is this a time when you need to return to the Lord Almighty? Only you know that! Renew your time with Him…read a Psalm today…read a Proverb based on the calendar day of the month. Pray intentionally for your family…for God to continue to reveal himself to you so that you will know who He is. And then, THANK HIM for everything you have and for His working in you life to make you more like Christ.

> **Will you not revive us again, that your people may rejoice in you? Show us your unfailing love, O LORD, and grant us your salvation.**

PSALM 85:6-7

I am old enough to have participated in many old time revivals. You don't hear and see as many of these types of revival meetings in today's churches. I guess you can say that man has progressed past the need for revival. I strongly disagree. There is a real need for true revival to occur, but I don't think the method should be the same as the old time revivals.

Modern man has moved to a more individualistic philosophy of living. This is where I think Satan has played a major role in damaging man's relationship with God and other people. We believe the lie that, "I'll do my thing, and you do your thing; just don't bother me." It's a shame but that's where the world is today. Social networking is stronger than ever, but it is predominantly through electronic devices. There is very little meeting face to face.

The world has also become very small. There is so much information that is now available to everyone through networking. A person's thinking about how to live their lives has become very private. They can share general information about themselves (including pictures), but don't get involved with religion.

For example, several years ago, the church I attend had a program to start Bible studies in neighborhoods. There were some nice signs to promote the studies that you could place in your front yard. Not more than a day went by when I received an anonymous note in my mailbox from a neighbor saying that he was offended by the sign and told me to remove it. I removed it so that I would not potentially harm a future opportunity to relate to that person.

If this is the norm for people today, how can you ever expect a revival to occur? God has His ways, and they usually involve judgment. It is my opinion that God will judge and there will be revival in the hearts of many people. When that happens, the verse above is a great prayer to God.

As Christian men, we need to be prepared by experiencing revival in our own lives, and I think it should happen at least once per year. Anything can bring on your revival, but you have to ask God for it and expect it. The following is what will happen to you.

"REVIVE"... after trudging along week after week through the rat race of this world, doesn't it sound good that God will revive you? A drink of water can revive you on a hot day...think of the person who created water reviving you.

"REJOICE"... great word for the feeling we experience when relieved of a burden, illness, or getting through a crisis.

"UNFAILING LOVE"... the love that only God can give you, because He is always eternally faithful.

"SALVATION"... from not only what this world can throw at you but also the salvation from being judged by God for all of your sins.

Please pray that you will experience revival in your spiritual life. Ask the Holy Spirit to change your focus from yourself, your problems, and this world to the one and only true living God. Those people who experience this revival will be different...the Holy Spirit will make that happen. Then you will be able to see others as God sees them, and reach out to them with His love.

52

Your Eternal life
Heaven or Lake of fire?

And the Word of God says:

"The day of the LORD is near for all nations. As you have done, it will be done to you; your deeds will return upon your own head."

OBADIAH 15

Wow! This is a real cheer me up verse. And it is full of joy for Believers, but, not so for unbelievers.

I believe that the "day of the Lord" is not a literal day but extends over one thousand years at least. It is packed full of events that will occur as part of the end times of our earth. One major event is the Second Coming of Christ. A fundamental truth about Christianity is that the Lord Jesus Christ will return to earth. This truth is repeated over and over in the Bible and is one of the most accepted facts about the future. No one knows the date or time other than God. Many people have tried and are still trying to predict when this cataclysmic event will occur. But, no one will be able to.

The "day of the Lord" can actually be a lengthy amount of time as the Bible is not clear on the length of certain events. For example, one event that most Believers are looking forward to is called the "rapture" (see 1 Thessalonians 4 for more details.) Basically, in the twinkling of an eye, every Believer will be "caught up" (Greek word for rapture) in the air with Jesus Christ. Some think that this will usher in the end times, but there may be other events that do that. After the rapture, there is a seven-year period during which a one-ruler government will be established on earth. The Bible does not speak of how much time elapses between the rapture and the seven-year period. The bottom line is that when it comes to end times, the timing of events becomes very hard to predict.

In the verse above, the day of the Lord is near. The way I look at it is that for every day that passes, we are one day closer to the day of the Lord. Also, note that this includes all the nations of the world. Events will occur that will impact the entire earth. Of course, there will be judgment. This happens near the end of the day of the Lord (see Revelation 19.)

God will judge every single person one at a time. Those who have accepted Jesus Christ as their Lord and Savior will have the blood of Christ covering their sins when God judges them. In other words, your sins were judged by God when Christ was on the cross. Therefore, Believers will pass into heaven as sinless human beings. Revelation 19 speaks of the events surrounding this judgment. It says that Believers will not face the second death. The first death was your physical death. You will not die again.

However, unbelievers will go through the first death (physical) and the second death (separation from God forever). Each unbeliever will stand before the Great White Throne and give an accounting for the deeds of their life. For every "good" thing that the unbeliever mentions, God will show them some "sin" they did. The unbeliever can stand before God for as long as he wants giving an account of his earthly deeds, but God will always find unforgiven sin in their life. God cannot allow a sinner into heaven. After the unbeliever has exhausted everything that they thought would get them into heaven, they will bow down at the name of Christ realizing the sinner that they are, and finally recognizing who Christ is. God will then cast them into the lake of fire (the second death) to be separated from God for eternity.

If you think your deeds are good enough to undo your sinfulness, then you do not understand Revelation 19. Read it carefully. Only the blood of Christ is sufficient for your sins to be removed from you forever. Get to know who Jesus is today. Know that God has made you as righteous as Jesus by making a way for all of your sins to be judged and for you to receive righteousness from God. This is how someone gets into heaven: by not doing anything themselves and trusting in the blood of Christ. Is this what you are doing? Or, do you have your own way to get into heaven that includes all the good things that you have done and, therefore, you do not need a Savior like Jesus Christ? Let me say that you are going the wrong way on a one-way street.

Today, make a decision to trust Jesus Christ to bring you into heaven because of His blood that He shed on the cross. Your life will never be the same.

CONCLUSION

In *Life-Changing Verses About Men*, I have provided Christian men with a unique "devotional" book. However, I do not want it referred to as a devotional book due to its emphasis on real and practical application of God's Word to the lives of Christian Men. It would be my goal that there are certain chapters that you might find convicting and will read and study those chapters on a yearly basis. We all need to be reminded of certain things in our life that relate to loving God and loving others. I hope that all of the *Life-Changing Verses* books will help you do that.

I also hope that Believers who read *Life-Changing Verses About Men* will be encouraged to read and study their Bible more in-depth. I know this is probably not the case with most Bible scholars, but I think that God's story is in every verse of the Bible. I know some verses would be really tough to see God's story, but I believe it is possible. This makes God's Word so exciting to realize that He provided the words that we read in the Bible, and every verse has something to say to us.

I plan to write *Life-Changing Verses Volume 4* in 2014. I also plan to write *Life-Changing Verses About God*. This is a book that I have not been able to find and wish that I had the opportunity to read about God in short chapters such as the book will be. I welcome any other specific groups that may fit into the context of *Life-Changing Verses*. Please email me with your suggestions. I will take your suggestion under consideration for future books.

After teaching through the Bible 7 times over 14 years, God has given me a perspective of His spiritual realm and Satan's current rule over the earth. I will leave you with the knowledge that Satan's rule is on borrowed time. Jesus will return and everything will change to God's glory and His purpose.

As Paul said in his letters, he wanted to go on to be with the Lord (i.e., die), but God had plans for him on this earth. I too want to go on to be with the Lord, and I have told Him so. But, that is up to Him and in the mean time, I grow more and more excited each day realizing that we are one day closer to seeing Christ appear.

My writings reflect this kind of thinking, because I believe God's Word as the ultimate and authoritative TRUTH about life. When talking with others, it is easy to identify Christians who have not made the Second Coming of Christ a part of the way they live. I think they are missing God's blessing that He gave us from Genesis through Revelation.

I encourage you to let me know your true thoughts about this book. Let me know your favorite ones and the ones that you felt conviction from the Holy Spirit. I also invite anyone to ask any question they may have about the Bible. Send them to me at carltonlcv@gmail.com.

LIST OF BIBLE VERSES USED

OLD TESTAMENT		NEW TESTAMENT	
Genesis 1:26–27	2	Matthew 5:27–28	32
Genesis 2:7	2	Matthew 6:1–4	29
Genesis 2:18, 20–25	3	Matthew 6:1–4	29
Genesis 2:21–24	35	Matthew 6:27	24
Genesis 3:8, 11–12	4	Matthew 6:9–20	12
Genesis 3:16–19	5	Matthew 6:27	24
Numbers 6:24–26	12	Matthew 11:28–29	30
		Matthew 18:6	36
Deuteronomy 4:39	28	Mark 8:34–37	21
Judges 2:10–12	14	Luke 18:15–18	36
1 Samuel 15:22–23	41	John 10:10	27
1 Kings 8:27	15	John 14:6	1
Job 40:8	46	Romans 6:1–4	19
Psalm 30:10	3		
Psalm 54:4	3		
Psalm 85:6–7	51	Romans 12:1–2	9
Psalm 119:15–16	49	2 Corinthians 2:14–16	26
Proverbs 13:24	36	Ephesians 4:26–27	31
Proverbs 14:29	31	Ephesians 5:21–23	34
Proverbs 27:17	40		
Proverbs 28:14	16	Ephesians 6:1–4	37

		Philippians 4:8	37
Proverbs 29:17	36	Colossians 3:16	22
Ecclesiastes 3:11	48	1 Thessalonians 1:3	13
Ecclesiastes 5:1-2	38	1 Timothy 6:17-19	25
Isaiah 44:13-20	23	Hebrews 11:24-28	17
Jeremiah 29:11	42	Hebrews 12:4-8	37
Hosea 11:8-9	20	James 1:5	18
Joel 2:12	6	1 Peter 1:18-19	8
Obadiah 15	52	1 Peter 3:14-16	39
Micah 6:8	50	2 Peter 3:18	44
Habakkuk 3:2	7	2 Peter 3:18	45
Haggai 1:5-7	47	1 John 2:15-17	10
Zechariah 1:3	51	1 John 2:15-17	11
Zechariah 10:2	33	1 John 4:16-18	43

INDEX OF MAJOR TOPICS

Finally, brothers,
whatever is true,
whatever is noble,
whatever is right,
whatever is pure,
whatever is lovely,
whatever is admirable –
if anything is excellent or praiseworthy –
think about such things.

Philippians 4:8

INDEX

ACKNOWLEDGEMENTS

I APPRECIATE WEST BOW PRESS and Thomas Nelson for the opportunity to publish this book.

The staff and people of First Baptist Church, Cumming, GA have truly lived up to the "church that gives itself away." Over the years, they have supported *Life-Changing Verses* and given constant feedback and encouragement to me.

Of particular note is Dr. Lou Meier who, on many long walks, discussed and debated the weekly *Life Changing Verses.* Dr. Meier was also instrumental in encouraging me to publish *Life-Changing Verses.*

My family has always been supportive throughout this work, and I thank them for their encouragement.

And, finally, my wife (D'Ette) of 44 years has been there throughout the writing of each book. She was involved in reading, reviewing, and offering constructive suggestions. She has met my every need. God has blessed me beyond anything I could think to ask for in my wife, D'Ette. She is my wife and my very best friend. And, she is extremely patient with me.

About the Author

CARLTON LEE ARNOLD HAS HAD a wide experience of teaching the Bible and reviewing numerous Christian curriculums. He served in the USAF for seven years. After retiring from Verizon in 2003, he worked five years on staff at First Baptist Church, Cumming, GA as Director of Adult Discipleship. He and his wife have lived in Georgia, Texas, Alabama, Missouri, Florida, and New York that has given them a wide perspective of different churches.

He now lives with his family in close proximity in the Atlanta, GA area.

Any comments or suggestions can be sent to carltonlcv@gmail.com.